ABOUT THE AUTHOR

Ruth Kelly is a practising social worker in Wexford. She has broad experience and expertise in all aspects of adoption, including adoption reunion. She has been involved in policy formation, research and training in adoption for the past ten years.

MOTHERHOOD SILENCED

The Experiences of Natural Mothers on Adoption Reunion

Ruth J.A. Kelly

The Liffey Press
Dublin

Published by
The Liffey Press Ltd
Ashbrook House, 10 Main Street
Raheny, Dublin 5, Ireland
www.theliffeypress.com

A catalogue record of this book is
available from the British Library.

ISBN 1-904148-72-7

Printed in Ireland by Colour Books

CONTENTS

10: Discussion (3): Life After Reunion —
    Reflections on a Lifetime of Loss 165

11: Conclusion 179

Postscript 191

Appendix 1 193

Appendix 2 198

Appendix 3 199

Bibliography 203

PREFACE

The mother who relinquished her child through adoption has long been the forgotten part of the adoption circle. Until recently, it was expected that these mothers would forget about the child whom they had relinquished and that they would continue with their lives as if their child did not exist. It was presumed that they would never want to know what happened to their child, nor ever want to meet their child again.

For many mothers this was not their experience. They were unable to forget their baby and their wish was always that they would, sometime in the future, have a chance to meet and have a reunion with their child.

This study examines the experience of a group of mothers who have had a reunion with their child who had been placed for adoption. The emotional experience of adoption and reunion and how it impacted on their lives is told through the mothers' own accounts of their experience.

All of the mothers had their reunions facilitated through an adoption agency. Issues in relation to the practice of adoption agencies and the services offered to the mothers are examined. The policies and practices of agencies which the mothers found helpful or unhelpful are outlined.

Adoption goes beyond the legal life of the contract signed at the time of relinquishment. For natural mothers it has life-long consequences which impact on reunion and beyond. This study records these experiences from the point of view of natural mothers.

ACKNOWLEDGEMENTS

There are many people — social work colleagues, friends and acquaintances — who have contributed to this study through their knowledge and experience of adoption, reunion and research. I would like to thank them and to let them know how grateful I have been for their time and generous support throughout the project.

I would like to thank Noreen Kearney, my thesis supervisor, for her constant direction and assistance throughout the research process. Her encouragement and attention to detail were invaluable and much appreciated at every stage of the project.

Thank you also to Dr Mary Corcoran whose knowledge and enthusiasm helped initiate the study and whose support and friendship ensured that I was able to bring it both to completion and to publication.

I would also like to thank the South Eastern Health Board who assisted me with sponsorship for the study.

I wish to gratefully acknowledge the financial support of An Bord Uchtála and the Department of Social Studies, Trinity College, which has helped to bring this study to publication.

This study is dedicated to the mothers who relinquished their children for adoption. Their courage has been an inspiration to me and from them I have learned a great deal.

Chapter 1

INTRODUCTION

The purpose of the research done for this book was to study the adoption reunions of a sample of mothers who relinquished their child for adoption. It is important that we know, from the point of view of the mothers directly involved, how the process of reunion has worked for them and how it has affected their lives.

The study explores the consequences of adoption and reunion from the point of view of the mothers who surrendered their child. It provides an insight into their reasons for initiating a search and tracing process which led to reunion, or their reasons for agreeing to meet the child when a reunion was requested. It describes how the experience of relinquishment, adoption and reunion has been for these mothers. The way in which the natural mothers perceive and experience the relationships which have developed with their children in the aftermath of reunion are also described.

Attitudes to Non-marital Pregnancy

All of the women who took part in this study were single at the time of pregnancy. Historically, attitudes in Ireland towards women who became pregnant outside marriage have been harsh and unforgiving. In the eighteenth and nineteenth centuries the stigmatisation of women who were pregnant or who gave birth outside marriage arose as a result of a rigid religious moral code which was adhered to in society during this period. For instance, commentators of the time often used the rate of illegitimacy as one of their indices of the moral state of the nation, and so an increase in illegitimate births was considered to be another step on the path to moral decay (Laslett, 1980).

The stigma attached to being pregnant outside marriage, or to being a single mother, continued, according to O'Hare et al. (1983) through the nineteenth and into the twentieth century. Single pregnant women and unmarried mothers and their children were often accommodated in workhouses which had been established under the Irish Poor Relief Act (1838), and which provided shelter and sustenance for the country's poor and destitute. Unmarried mothers were frequently obliged to remain for a long time in these workhouses, as they had no alternative accommodation because of their lack of acceptance by family or the community (O'Hare et al., 1983).

In the report of the Commission on the Relief of the Sick and Destitute Poor in 1927, Powell (1992) notes that the Commissioners revealed a particularly patriarchal attitude towards single mothers. The report advocated a series of recommendations that effectively conferred a criminal status on single women with children born out of wedlock. One of the recommendations of the Commission was that single mothers should be divided into two classes: those who were amenable to reform (generally women who had just one illegitimate child); and those who had to be regarded as less hopeful cases (generally women who had more than one illegitimate child and/or extra-marital children). The Commissioner's report noted that the state had in fact no legal power to detain a woman in any Poor Law Institution, but suggested that this should be changed. Their recommendation was that institutions should have the power to detain a single woman after her first pregnancy for one year: detention for two years was recommended in the case of a woman who had a second pregnancy.

A further recommendation of the Commission was that separate institutions should be established to offer accommodation and assistance to single mothers as workhouses were generally considered to be unsuitable for them. There was already a prototype institution of this kind in Cork, opened by the Sisters of the

Sacred Heart of Jesus and Mary in 1922. This institution was, according to the report of the Department of Local Government and Public Health, "intended primarily for young mothers who have fallen for the first time and who were likely to be influenced towards a useful and respectable life" (Powell, 1992). For single mothers who already had more than one illegitimate child, the Commissioners' proposals were quickly put into effect through a co-operative effort of church and state. By 1932 an arrangement had been established between the Local Authorities and the Sisters-in-Charge of Magdalen Asylums in Dublin and other parts of the country for the containment of women who were experiencing what was considered to be this "more intractable problem" (Powell, 1992). The attitudes towards single pregnant women and single mothers which prevailed in both the Magdalen Asylums and Mother and Baby Homes at this time were extremely harsh, judgemental and rigid. The women who availed of the accommodation and services were often treated very cruelly and the institutions were often run more like penitentiaries than nursing homes (O'Hare et al., 1983; Powell, 1992; Goulding, 1998; Cooney, 1999). Goulding (1998), who worked as a midwife in one such Mother and Baby Home in the 1950s, related her impressions of the kind of place it was:

> The girls were treated like criminals in this building and there was a general air of penitence. It permeated every corner — even the chapel. Those in charge who ran the godforsaken place like a prison did so as cruelly and as uncaringly as any medieval gaoler.

As a rule, the severe and judgemental attitudes towards women who became pregnant outside marriage or towards women who were caring for their illegitimate child permeated the ethos of many state and church agencies. Church and State were wedded in their conceptualisation of unmarried motherhood as problematic. In the 1950s for example, women who were pregnant outside marriage were described by one of the prominent social welfare agencies, the Catholic Social Welfare Bureau, as "fallen women" and "grave sinners" (quoted in Cooney, 1999). At around the same period (1956), a child care officer who worked directly with single mothers and with problem families wrote in the Catholic publication *Christus Rex*:

> . . . it is not unfair to generalise and say that the girl who has the illegitimate child very often comes from an unsatisfactory family background and as a result of this has developed a neurotic character — the illegitimate baby being in the nature of a symptom of her psychological ill-health (Kenny, 1956, quoted in Skehill, 1999).

As a result of this morally damning attitude towards non-marital pregnancy, many single pregnant women travelled to England in order to have their babies there (Powell, 1992; Callanan, 2002). This raised problems of its own for the English authorities as the church and social services in many cities were unable to cope with the numbers arriving (Callanan, 2002). Commenting in the 1960s on how this flight to England further demonstrated the cruel and severe attitude towards single pregnant women in Ireland, Viney (1964) quotes a British social worker:

> . . . the fear of these girls has to be seen to be believed . . . what sort of society do you have in Ireland that puts the girls into this state? (Viney, 1964)

And some eight years later, in 1972, the situation for single pregnant woman and unmarried mothers continued to be difficult. At a conference in Kilkenny in 1972 on the "Unmarried Mother in the Irish Community", attention was drawn to the fact that the attitudes in Irish society towards extra-marital pregnancy were still extremely judgemental. The report of the conference included the following statement:

> . . . these women are regarded as second class citizens and very often their misfortune is interpreted as being of their own devising (Report of the National Conference on Community Services for the Unmarried Parent, 1972).

That having a child outside marriage was, in 1972, still conceptualised as "misfortune" implicitly speaks volumes about the prevailing culture in relation to unmarried mothers up to the early 1970s.

Adoption Law

Legal adoption was introduced into Ireland in 1952 with the passing of the Adoption Act (1952). Prior to that date, children had been informally adopted by couples, but these arrangements had no legal status.

Eligibility for adoption was defined in Section 10 of the Act which laid down the conditions necessary to permit the legal adoption of a child as follows:

"An adoption order shall not be made unless the child –

    a.   resides in the State, and

    b.   is, at the date of application, not less than six months and not more than seven years of age, and

    c.   is illegitimate or an orphan."

Eligibility to adopt was defined in Section 11 where the Act stated:

"11. (1) An adoption order shall not be made unless –

    a.   the applicants are a married couple who are living together, or

    b.   the applicant is the mother or natural father or a relative of the child, or

    c.   the applicant is a widow."

In relation to the eligibility requirements of adopters Section 12 of the Act went on to state:

"12.(1) An adoption order shall not be made unless the conditions of this section in regard to religion are fulfilled.

(2) The applicant or applicants shall be of the same religion as the child and his parents, or if the child is illegitimate, his mother."

And in relation to the suitability of adopters Section 13 of the Act stated:

"13.(1) The Board shall not make an adoption order unless satisfied that the applicant is of good moral character, has sufficient means to support the child and is a suitable person to have parental rights and duties in respect of the child.

(2) Where the applicants are a married couple, the Board shall satisfy itself as to the moral character and suitability of each of them."

The Adoption Act gave effect to an Adoption Order which established the legal relationship between an adopter and an adopted child. The Adoption Order also had the purpose of severing the legal relationship between the mother who gave birth and her child. In relation to the severing of the relationship between a mother and her child Section 24 of the Act stated:

"Upon an adoption order being made:

a. the child shall be considered with regard to the rights and duties of parents and children in relation to each other as the child of the adopter or adopters born to him, her, or them in lawful wedlock;

b. the mother or guardian shall lose all parental rights and be freed from all parental duties with respect to the child."

Adoption legislation in Ireland thus gave all rights and duties with regard to the child to the adopting parents, and obliged the natural mother to relinquish these rights and duties. Effectively, the 1952 Act reflected the social mores and beliefs of the time it was drawn up.

As part of his analysis of church and state in modern Ireland, Whyte (1980) suggested that there were four main reasons for the growth of pressure to introduce legal adoption in Ireland:

1. The rise in illegitimate births which reached an all time high of 3.99 per cent in the years 1944–46.

2. A changing social climate which embraced the idea that children would be better raised in families rather than institutions.

3. Pressure from parents who cared for boarded out and foster children and who wished to adopt these children.

4. Economic considerations which were voiced by Local Authorities who were responsible for the costs of maintenance of boarded out children. Adoption was favoured by these authorities as a no-cost alternative to institutional or boarded out care.

The introduction of legal adoption had been sought for a number years. The Adoption Society (Ireland), an organisation which included people from many walks of life, was the main pressure group which was calling for legislation. The Joint Committee of Women's Societies and Social Workers took up the question in 1938, and the Irish Trade Union Congress passed a resolution of support in 1949 (Whyte, 1980).

The government did not initially support the introduction of adoption. Through the Minister for Justice it gave the following reasons for its opposition: 1) the position of parents was already given ample protection under the law; and 2) it was unjust and unchristian to deprive a natural mother irrevocably of all rights over her child. Whyte (1980) pointed out two further strong objections to introducing adoption, viz. a strongly held feeling, particularly in rural areas, that "property should go to someone of one's own blood" and the fear that it would facilitate proselytism. The debate went on for a number of years (1937–52), and eventually, through negotiation and the introduction of a clause which required the adopting parents to be of the same religion as the child's mother, the objections subsided and the Adoption Act was passed in 1952.

Natural Mothers and Adoption

In Ireland during the 1950s, 1960s, and 1970s the majority of children born outside marriage were placed for adoption (Adoption Board, Annual Report 1999). Little recognition was given to the needs of the women who relinquished their children and generally they were not afforded a service from agencies in the aftermath of relinquishment (Darling, 1974). In Ireland, and in other countries, the expectation appeared to be that the mother, who had relinquished all rights and responsibilities, would disappear and forever remain anonymous (Inglis, 1984; Howe et al., 1992). Social approval was given to the adoptive parents who took on all rights and responsibilities for the child (Whyte, 1980; Inglis, 1984; Howe et al., 1992; O'Halloran, 1992). A natural mother's act of relinquishing all of her rights and responsibilities was interpreted as an act through which she would deny and silence her motherhood. Any wish or need that she might have to know what happened to her child was not recognised or part of the contract.

Changing Attitudes

For many years after the introduction of the 1952 Act it would appear that little if any consideration was given to the possibility that an adopted child might at a later stage of its life, as a matter of right, seek information on its background. Neither was it ever envisaged that the mother who gave birth would wish to have contact with or meet her child. According to the report of the Review Committee on Adoption (1984), "this practice was shaped by the prevailing view and attitudes of the time, and represented what was acceptable not only for the natural parents, but also for the adoptive parents, and to professionals in the field".

In 1984, the report of the Review Committee on Adoption suggested that "the adoption laws and procedures (in Ireland) had evolved on the basis of anonymity and confidentiality". The Review Committee however also noted through submissions which had been made to its report that attitudes to the secrecy attached to adoption were changing. The submissions calling for change — i.e. the release of information in relation to birth identity, were coming from adopted people — and in relation to a wish to make contact with relinquished children, from natural parents.

Agencies and organisations involved in adoption started to note the growing interest of adopted people in having information about their birth history in the 1980s (Lefroy, 1987). In the 1990s, social workers involved in adoption in the Eastern Health Board called for legislation and a new policy to allow search and reunion for birth parents and adopted people to take place in a structured and regulated manner (Eastern Health Board, Internal Document, 1990). In 1992 Barnardos Adoption Advice Service in Dublin called for "the right of access of adopted people to their birth records" (Gibbons, 1992). The Adoption Advice Service of Barnardos also noted a steady increase in enquiries in relation to search and reunion (Gibbons, 1992).

In its annual report of 1994, the Adoption Board called for the establishment of a National Contact Register and asked that the question of access to birth records be addressed through legislation. Also in 1994, the Council of Irish Adoption Agencies, which represented all registered adoption agencies, called for legislation to give natural parents and adopted persons access to identifying information and a full and comprehensive tracing and reunion service (Council of Irish Adoption Agencies, 1994). In 1994 the government published their health plan, "Shaping a Healthier Future: A Strategy for Effective Health Care in the 1990s", in which a commitment was made to:

> . . . provide arrangements to facilitate contact between
> adopted persons and their birth parents, including the
> establishment of a Contact Register.

In their Information Handbook, published in 1998, the Adoptive
Parents Association of Ireland welcomed the promised national
Contact Register, recognising that "at some stage, many adopted
people and many birth mothers decide they would like to find out
more about themselves or each other". In their annual report of
1998, the Adoption Board also welcomed the Minister of Health's
commitment to the introduction of search and reunion legislation
and asked that it be given priority in their legislative programme.
The Adoption Board repeated their request in their Annual Report
of 1999 as, in the meantime, no legislation had emerged.

In 1993 an important High Court judgment had been handed
down in relation to the release of birth certificates of persons who
were adopted. This judgment determined that where an adopted
person was seeking information under Section 22 (5) of the Adoption Act (1952), the Adoption Board was obliged to inform itself
about the circumstances of the individual case and to decide
whether to release or withhold the information sought. Part of this
process entailed the adopted person being offered counselling, the
purpose of which was to explain the possible outcome and consequences of their receiving identifying information in relation to
their birth identity. It also involved initiating enquiries to ascertain the whereabouts and circumstances of the mother who gave
birth, and if possible to determine her attitude to the release of
information sought. Once all the information had been gathered
by the Adoption Board, the Board was obliged to make a decision
as to whether it was appropriate and proper to make an order to
release information under the Adoption Act 1952.

In 1999, 45 birth certificates identifying the natural mother
were released by the Board to adopted people. On the other hand,
for natural mothers, *no* legal channel was provided through which
they could obtain information about a child who was relinquished
for adoption.

Search and Reunion: The Present Service

The facilitation of reunions is a relatively new phenomenon in Ireland. In 2001 there were no national statistics collated by any statutory body in relation to the total number of tracing and search enquires made of the Adoption Board and the 13 registered adoption societies. Neither were there any national statistics collated on the number of reunions which have taken place. There is no complete national database on what is happening in the field of adoption reunion. As a result it is impossible to have an accurate or complete statistical picture of what has happened in the past or what is happening at present in relation to search and reunion.

Despite there being no legal framework or legal entitlement for natural mothers to search and trace, all 13 registered adoption agencies and the Adoption Board offer tracing, search and reunion services to natural mothers. As there are no national guidelines in relation to the procedures and policies to be followed, each agency has developed its own polices, procedures and guidelines as to how they will initiate a search.[1]

The general procedures which all agencies follow however are broadly similar and include the following steps:

- Upon approaching an agency requesting a tracing and reunion service a natural mother will be offered counselling in relation to the issues involved and the possible consequences of tracing and reunion.

---

[1] The Council of Irish Adoption Agencies, which represents all Irish adoption agencies, produced their proposed "Guidelines for Policy and Disclosure in Relation to Search" in 1997. Whereas many of the proposals in these guidelines were taken up by individual agencies, they were not adopted across the board and so each agency in fact continued to operate their own individual guidelines and policies. The Adoption Board is presently in the process of writing a policy and procedures manual and has sought the assistance of the Council of Irish Adoption Agencies in doing so. There is, however, no indication of a completion or publication date available.

- Non-identifying information about her child who was adopted will be shared with her from the agency file (e.g. child's new first name, some details about the adoptive parents and family, province or area of the country to which they were adopted.)

- The agency will then undertake to try to contact the adopted person in order to ascertain if they are open to contact and possibly reunion.

- If the adopted person refuses contact the mother is informed of this fact and the agency will indicate to her that they cannot proceed any further as they have to respect the wishes of the person who was adopted. If, on the other hand, the adopted person agrees to contact, the form of contact (letters, phone calls, meetings) is negotiated with him or her.

- The adopted person's wishes are relayed to the natural mother and the reunion process proceeds from there.

At this point, agencies provide differing levels of service. The service can range from the use of the office of the agency as an intermediary address through which correspondence is routed, right through to actually facilitating the reunion meeting. In the event of reunion, it is the policy of agencies to offer post-reunion support or counselling to the parties involved.

In 2005 (subsequent to this study having been completed), a National Contact Register has been established by the Adoption Board. This Register will connect mothers and children separated by adoption provided that *both* are open and willing to have contact. As the Register was only established in 2005, its services were not available to the mothers who took part in this study.

Aims of this Study

At the time of writing there has been no published research on adoption reunion in Ireland. Biographical accounts of adoption and relinquishment make reference to reunion, but do not expand in any great detail on the experience (Collins, 1993; Batts, 1994). There is no central collection of statistics on the numbers of reunions taking place, nor is there any information being collated nationally on how reunions were initiated or what has been their outcome. It appeared important and worthwhile therefore to undertake research into this phenomenon.

At the outset the aims of this study were:

1. To provide information on how the reunion of natural mothers with their children affected the mothers who had relinquished. The particular experience of reunion for natural mothers in Ireland had never previously been recorded. The question as to whether the experience had been similar to that of mothers in other countries arose and was of interest.

2. To discover what were the positive and negative aspects of reunion for natural mothers and to determine how post-reunion relationships had developed.

3. To enquire as to what had been the effect of adoption on the lives of mothers who had relinquished a child in an Irish context. Research in other countries had found that the effects and consequences of adoption had been negative and long lasting for natural mothers.

4. To establish if the procedures for arranging reunions were satisfactory for natural mothers. At present the vast majority of adoption reunions in Ireland are facilitated through registered adoption agencies.

Structure of the Study

The remainder of this study is divided into ten further chapters. Chapter 2 provides background information by reviewing published research and literature on adoption and reunion. Chapter 3 outlines the methodology of the study, identifying how the respondents were recruited, the interviews and the process of analysis. Chapters 4–7 contain the findings and the respondents' own accounts of their experience of adoption and reunion. Chapters 8–10 discuss the findings and compare them with published research on adoption reunions which have been carried out in other countries. Chapter 11 draws conclusions from the findings.

Chapter 2

BACKGROUND

A review of the research specifically on adoption and on adoption reunions from the perspective of natural mothers reveals that there has been relatively little undertaken on this topic worldwide. To date, no research on the subject has been published in Ireland.

One possible reason for the shortage of research on reunion from the natural mother's perspective, according to a number of authors, could be that natural mothers tended to be the silent and unseen part of the adoption circle. The fact that the birth and adoption of their child was often a secret shared not at all or only with a trusted few has meant that the stories and accounts of these women were hidden. A number of authors have pointed to how these stories and accounts were not part of the public discourse as a real event in an ordinary woman's life (Howe, Sawbridge and Hinings, 1992; Wells, 1994; Wadia-Ells, 1996; Robinson, 2000).

Another possible explanation put forward by researchers on the topic is that it is only within the last quarter of a century that studies have emerged which point to a growing interest by adopted people in tracing their natural parents. Their motive for doing this is to learn more for themselves about their birth heritage and the reason why they were placed for adoption. As a result there has been a recognition that the exchange of information and a possible reunion between a child who had been placed for adoption and a natural mother might be an important part of the adoption process (Pacheco and Eme, 1993; Feast et al., 1994; Iredale, 1997; Howe and Feast, 2000).

The dearth of research has also been attributed to the fact that adoption was seen as a relatively simple event: a mother gave up her child for adoption and her child was raised by adoptive parents as their own child without any significant or substantial reference to birth heritage. The mother who had given birth and who had parted with her child had no role to play and was a silent party to the adoption story. The natural mother's life-long loss of her child and the resultant grief that she might have experienced were not recognised as part of the process of adoption. As a number of authors have identified, the natural mother was rarely referred to or spoken about by anyone involved in the adoption process (Watson, 1986; Silverman, 1988; Howe et al., 1992).

The fact that legally, adoption was a closed and confidential process may also be a factor as to why there has been little research on relinquishment and reunion. Not only was information not available to natural mothers, adopted people and adoptive parents, but access to adoption files within agencies, save for purely statistical purposes, was not encouraged. In Ireland a further measure in reducing the accessibility of information on adoption was the restriction placed on the release of information in relation to adoption under the Freedom of Information Act 1997.

A final possible reason which has been put forward as to why there has been so little research on reunion may be because reunions are very personal, individualised events which the participants might not want to have examined and discussed in the public domain. The fact that the phenomenon of reunion is relatively recent and that its historical context is shrouded in secrecy and silence may also add to a reluctance by natural mothers to expose the details of such a private and stigmatising event.

When seeking to establish what research and literature had been published on the topic of adoption reunions for purposes of this study, a review was undertaken of Irish, British, American, Canadian and Australian journals of the social sciences. The internet was also explored under the general headings "adoption", "birth mother", "natural mother", "adoptee", "adoption reunion" and "adoptive parents". Further texts in relation to adoption and reunion were sourced through libraries, bookstores and organisations which ran support groups for natural mothers.

The literature which emerged on the topic of natural mothers and how they were affected by adoption can be divided into five categories:

1. Qualitative and quantitative research studies on mothers who relinquished a child for adoption, with discussion and analysis of how they have coped in the years post-relinquishment.

2. Qualitative and quantitative studies on mothers who have had a reunion with the child they placed for adoption, with analysis and discussion of the reunion process and its aftermath.

3. Biographical accounts of the experience of adoption for natural mothers which form part of the general texts on adoption.

4. Autobiographies by mothers who relinquished their children which included detailed accounts of how parting with a child affected them, and how they experienced reunion.

5. Texts which offer advice and information about reunions and which also contain accounts by natural mothers of their experience of adoption and reunion.

The justification and reasons for the research that has been published on mothers who relinquished children and who have had a reunion would appear to have been prompted by a number of factors. One factor was a realisation by professionals working with relinquishing mothers of their own lack of knowledge in relation to the experience and consequences of having parted with a child. Winkler and Van Keppel (1984), who undertook one of the first studies in Australia, stated that they wished to obtain information that would contribute to an understanding of the relinquishment process, and to determine why some women made a better adjustment to the relinquishment of their child than did others. The need to have a better understanding of the consequences of relinquishment was being expressed by social workers and psycholo-

gists who met with mothers who had presented to agencies requesting counselling in the aftermath of relinquishment.

In 1988, also in Australia, Petrina Slaytor, through her work in
adoption reunion at the Royal Hospital for Women, New South
Wales, found that there were many gaps in the information available to social workers whose work included counselling the various parties in the reunion process. It appeared that one obvious
way to start obtaining such data would be to ask those who had
already experienced such a reunion to record their knowledge
and understanding of what the process had been like for them.
When justifying her research, Slaytor (1988) states that at the time
there appeared to be no literature providing guidelines for the
preparation, conduct and follow-up of such reunions and one of
the main purposes of her study was to assist in providing such
guidelines.

Around the same time in the US, questions were being asked
by professionals in the field of search and reunion about the moti-
vation of people who sought reunions. In 1988 this led to a study
by Silverman, Campbell, Patti and Briggs Style. These researchers
sought to gather information on the aforementioned questions
and also the impact and consequences of reunion meetings on the
participants. In England nearly a decade later, McMillan and Irving (1997) in pursuit of further knowledge on the topic, sought to
establish what was the longer-term outcome of reunion for the
participants who had been through the process. Their research
enquired into how much reunion altered the way in which participants viewed themselves and their adoption experience, and
what the repercussions were for all of those affected.

Another factor which has led to the publication of research on
relinquishment and reunion has been the changing nature of
adoption practice. Changes in attitudes have led to a recognition
of the rights of adopted people to have information on their birth
identity. Such changing attitudes in Great Britain have, for example, led to the enactment of the Children Act 1975 (Section 26)
which gave adopted people in Great Britain opportunities to obtain information about their natural parents. According to Bouch-

ier, Lambert and Triseliotis (1991), this legislation led to an increasing number of mothers being encouraged to contact adoption agencies and social services. Mothers who had relinquished children were encouraged to make contact with agencies in order for agencies to obtain information for adopted adults who were seeking information. As a result of past adoption practice, there was often little information concerning natural mothers on agencies' files, and rarely was there up-to-date information as to her whereabouts. Legislation similar to that enacted in Great Britain was also enacted in other jurisdictions such as British Columbia, New South Wales and New Zealand. This legislation was enacted in the 1980s and 1990s and also led to the establishment of Adoption Contact Registers or state agencies with similar functions. The purpose of these Adoption Contact Registers has been to enable people separated through adoption to make contact through official, state-sponsored channels. Research into the functioning of three of these agencies (in New Zealand, British Columbia and England) has yielded data and information on the effects of relinquishment on natural mothers. It has also provided information on how mothers have fared since they placed their children for adoption, the effects of reunion for natural mothers and how the services provided through the registries have functioned.

All of the information gathered through these various research studies has enhanced our understanding of relinquishment, adoption and adoption reunion.

The publication of biographies and autobiographies that give direct accounts of the experience of adoption for natural mothers have also added greatly to our knowledge on adoption and reunion. These biographies have been justified by their authors as providing mothers with an opportunity to tell their own personal story of relinquishment and sometimes of reunion. Batts (1994) claims that her justification in publishing the account of her experience of adoption and reunion was in an effort, for herself, to come to some understanding of all that had happened in the years post-relinquishment. It was also her hope that her published story might be in some way helpful to other women who had experi-

enced the pain of adoption. Robinson (2000) states that her purpose in writing her own account is to identify and give recognition to the very specific loss experienced by mothers who relinquished their children for adoption.

Throughout the published research and literature on relinquishment and reunion there are a number of recurring themes
which are identified and explored by the authors. The main
themes which emerge are reviewed below.

Relinquishment and Loss

Howe, Sawbridge and Hinings (1992) suggest that thinking on
modern adoption has gone through two stages: in the first, adoption existed to satisfy the needs of the childless married woman;
in the second, the needs of the child were given prime consideration. In both instances, however, once the child had been placed
with the adopters, it was the story of the new family that was followed. The mother who had given birth was expected to do the
decent thing and disappear. Her silence was required. Her identity was concealed and her existence was often denied. There were
often no records about her or her history. The reasons for the
adoption decision were rarely recorded. There was no information kept on file as to where she could be contacted if any need
arose or if her child wished to do so. The denial of her existence
was, as Reinharz suggests, "socially constructed and a form of
oppression" (Reinharz, 1994).

The importance of re-claiming the identity of mothers who
had relinquished a child for adoption was highlighted for Inglis
(1984) when she was interviewing women in Australia as part of a
research study on reproduction. In her book she describes how
many of the women she interviewed revealed a long-held secret
in relation to their reproductive history. They had given birth out
of wedlock and had given up their child for adoption. Inglis
(1984) states that these women "exhibited a pattern of behaviour
in the telling which centred on an unresolved grief and an am-
bivalence about their motherhood". She noted that their isolation

in both the event and the memory was striking, and that their social identity as mothers had been silenced and unrecognised.

That the effect of relinquishment was experienced as a profound and long-lasting loss for a majority of natural mothers was a central theme to emerge in all of the literature on relinquishment and reunion. In addition, the loss experienced had a number of distinguishing features which interfered with any meaningful resolution of the loss. Condon (1986) states that the women in his study described the feelings of sadness, loss and depression at the time of relinquishment as being "intense" or "the most intense ever experienced". Bouchier et al. (1991) found that just over 90 per cent of their respondents identified relinquishment as a severely stressful event in their lives, and 50 per cent cited it as the most stressful event. Their sense of loss was "bleak and despairing". The mothers frequently made a comparison with death when they spoke of the adoption of their child. Silverman et al. (1988) found that 90 per cent of the respondents in their study reported their feelings of grief after the surrender of their child to have been worse than anticipated.

It is not hard to imagine how a mother, having just given birth, would have profound feelings of loss in the event of having to immediately part with her child. Millen and Roll (1985) suggest that in a society which defines women as mothers, mothers-to-be or childless, the woman who has given birth and then relinquished her child is an enigma. Having signed away her legal claim to the child, she is often perceived as the most unnatural of women, a rejecting mother. It was generally expected that a mother who relinquished her child had severed any emotional bond which had developed and gladly resumed her interrupted life (Millen and Roll, 1985; Watson, 1986; Robinson, 2000). However, the evidence which emerges from the literature on natural mothers demonstrates that, far from forgetting about her child's existence, mothers most often return to living their lives without the child but do so with much pain and anguish about having relinquished their child.

Grief and sadness are the expected responses to loss, and indeed are generally seen as beneficial responses in so much as they enable a person to process the loss which has occurred. Coming to terms with the loss of a child as a result of adoption, however, can be extremely difficult because of the unique nature of the loss. Robinson (2000) suggests that "adoption-related grief" has a number of distinct features which are particular to the experience of relinquishment. Millen and Roll (1985) suggested that "distorted mourning reactions" are a part of the experience of all mothers who relinquish a child for adoption.

One of the distinctive features of adoption-related loss that emerges in the literature on natural mothers is the on-going feelings of self-reproach experienced by mothers for having parted with their child. Winkler and Van Keppel (1984) found that natural mothers said they felt responsible for the decision to give up the child for adoption and therefore felt the loss as a self-inflicted one. Condon (1986) found that 80 per cent of his respondents reproached themselves for their act of relinquishment. These feelings of self-reproach often resulted in intense feelings of guilt and shame for being a party to the act of relinquishment. The mothers believed that their complicity had been required to enable the adoption to take place.

Soroksy (1978, quoted in Brodzinsky et al., 1990) states that his respondents expressed concern that their child would never forgive them for what might be seen as abandonment. As a result, they were often overwhelmed with feelings of guilt for what they had done. Bouchier et al. (1991) also note that their respondents reported continuing unhappiness and guilt arising from their loss. Mothers believed that their self-image was poor and that they had difficulties in relationships due to the silence and secrecy they had had to endure in relation to relinquishment. Robinson (2000) suggests that natural mothers often further reproached themselves for even continuing to have feelings for their child as the advice they had been given was that they would "get over it", that they should "get on with their lives" and that they should "put it all behind them". Robinson suggests that many mothers went on to have intense feelings of guilt but became apologetic about their feelings because they were contrary to what they had been advised would be their experience.

When describing the experience and nature of their loss through adoption, mothers have often referred to the sense of loss becoming intensified with the passage of time. Condon (1986) reports that mothers identified how "their loss was intensified through feelings of anger about being forced to part with their child". Watson (1986) suggests that this anger of natural mothers towards themselves and others cannot easily be alleviated because the mothers often feel there were things they might have done to prevent the loss. Bouchier et al. (1991) report how mothers said that in their loss they were haunted by memories that went "on and on". They recounted how they thought about their child at least every week, and often daily. Winkler and Van Keppel (1984) draw attention to how some mothers appeared to adjust to relinquishment better than others. In their study 50 per cent of the relinquishing mothers reported an increasing sense of loss, which they say extended over periods of 30 years. Their findings suggest that for the 50 per cent of mothers whose feelings of loss did not intensify in the aftermath of adoption the support of family and friends to whom they were able to talk and express their feelings about their loss was important. They appeared to make a better adjustment to their relinquishment than those who felt unsupported and kept the fact of their relinquishment private.

Finally, in relation to loss and relinquishment, a number of studies suggest that there may be a link between the natural mother's prolonged feelings of grief and the state of their mental health in the aftermath of relinquishment. Condon (1986) states in his conclusions that overall, results showed that relinquishing mothers had significantly higher scores on depression, psychosomatic symptoms and general psychological disability. Logan (1996), whose research was commissioned by the Mental Health Services in Manchester, found that mental health issues emerged for a substantial proportion of the women she interviewed. Her population of mothers was drawn from the After Adoption Service in Manchester, an organisation from which natural mothers had sought assistance. She states that 82 per cent of the women described depression as a significant factor in their lives. Logan (1996) suggests that this depression may arise out of a residue of guilt, loss and unresolved grief. Neither of these studies records a comparison with a control group of women who had not relinquished children, and as a result the significantly higher scores of mental health problems for mothers who had relinquished children must be treated with caution. It is important however to note that these mothers identified depression and general psychological disability as a factor in their lives; this may not have been their experience in the absence of not having parted with a child.

What emerges from an examination of the literature under the theme of loss in relation to relinquishment is that the advice which relinquishing mothers received "to start over and leave the past behind" was not consistent with their experience (Silverman et al., 1988; Howe et al., 1992). For the most part, time did not heal or lessen the pain for mothers who had parted with their child.

Disempowerment through Relinquishment

Though adoption was often cited as being the solution which was in the best interests of the child and of natural mothers, the research to date points to how natural mothers have in fact experienced adoption as a disempowering and traumatic event in their lives. The circumstances and pressures experienced by a single woman when she discovered she was pregnant were often intense. In Australia, Inglis (1984) describes how:

> . . . those of us who were girls during this time of sexual repression and rapid social change knew all about her, but we rarely saw her. She disappeared. Either into a hasty marriage or away to that vague place girls said to be "in trouble" went to.

For parents the horror of having a daughter who was pregnant outside marriage necessitated the immediate implementation of plans to hide the reality. Once the child was born, much of the literature describes how a harshly punitive attitude surrounded the unmarried mother and how the pressure to conform to the wishes of others in relation to a decision in favour of adoption were powerful and sometimes extreme (Watson, 1986; Inglis, 1984; Howe et al., 1992; Wells, 1994; Batts, 1994; Robinson, 2000). Howe et al. (1992) suggest that mothers often felt themselves "being channelled towards adoption by a determined gang of social, emotional and practical pressures". None of the research studies conclude that there is evidence to suggest that mothers were empowered and given a real choice in relation to a decision to part with their child.

A fairly commonly shared belief about adoption is that mothers freely choose to relinquish their children (Inglis, 1984). Despite this belief, the fact that relinquishing mothers did not believe they had *freely* chosen to relinquish their children is a central theme in much of the literature. In Australia, Winkler and Van Keppel (1984) found that 44 per cent of their respondents said that the relinquishment of their child was against their wishes with pressure from parents being cited as one of the main reasons for the adoption having taking place. Pressure from parents was also noted by mothers as a reason for parting with their child in other studies in England, the United States and Canada (Cotton and Parish, 1987; Silverman et al., 1988; Sullivan and Groden, 1995). In New Zealand, Field (1990) found that 70 per cent of mothers recalled getting little or no emotional support from family or friends at the time they became pregnant, which left them feeling that they had no choice about giving up their child for adoption.

Pressure from agencies and professionals within agencies to place non-marital children for adoption was a further disempowering measure which unmarried mothers often experienced. The belief that the ideal family of two married parents was essential for the moral and physical welfare of a child was often intimately connected to the pressure applied to single mothers to part with their child. This belief permeated the attitudes and practice of professionals and agencies who offered assistance to single pregnant women throughout the 1950s, 1960s and into the 1970s. Howe et al. (1992) relate how the views of doctors and midwives who are intimately involved in the birthing process can affect the mother. A single mother's achievements in the delivery room, having undergone the physical effort of having a baby, were often viewed with dismay rather than delight (Inglis, 1984; Howe et al., 1992; Goulding, 1998). Social workers often proffered views on what might be best for babies born outside marriage to vulnerable and unsupported mothers, with an emphasis on the fact that what was the best plan for the baby was adoption (Howe et al. 1992). Silverman et al. (1988) found that "many birth parents felt pressured by adoption agencies to surrender, and that many felt coerced into agreeing that they could or should not keep the baby". Sullivan et al. (1995) also noted that natural mothers identified pressure from agencies as one of the factors which made them feel they had to choose adoption for their child. To have two parents, who were married and who upheld the current moral code surrounding motherhood and parenting was, at the time, the policy aim promoted by agencies and professionals in the field, as being in the best interests of the welfare of the child (Bennet, 1976; Inglis, 1984; Howe et al., 1992; Triseliotis et al., 1997).

In the aftermath of relinquishment, the system of closed adoption (which appears to have been the type of adoption experienced by all of the women who feature in the various studies and texts reviewed for this study), was also characteristically disempowering for mothers. Closed adoption meant that once a mother had relinquished her child there was no possibility that she would be allowed to have information about her child in the aftermath of the signing of the adoption contract. She was invariably denied information about the new identity of her child and little or no information was shared with her about the adoptive parents. She rarely had any idea where in the country her child had been placed, and she had not been given any guarantees that if, for instance, her child were to die, she would be informed.

As a result of having no information in the years after they had parted with their child, mothers wondered and worried about what had happened to their child. The respondents in the study by Logan (1996) describe how they had feelings of "ongoing fear and anxiety" through not knowing what had happened to their child. Logan (1996) suggests that these overriding feelings seemed to drive their need to search for their child. Bouchier et al. (1991) note that mothers had a "special kind of anxiety" through not knowing about the welfare of their child; they suggest that this pining is the subjective and emotional component of the urge to search. Silverman et al. (1988) suggest that this lack of information about how their child was progressing may be a factor in the continuing and unresolved grief for relinquishing mothers. Mothers who relinquished children through adoption most often have been denied their identity as mothers. This denial of any news or information about the wellbeing of their child was yet a further way in which they were disempowered through the adoption process.

Despite having been involved in closed adoption, which by its very nature gave a natural mother no rights to contemplate the possibility of a reunion with her child, a central theme to emerge from the literature reviewed points to an ongoing yearning by natural mothers to have a reunion with their child. Sorosky (1978, quoted in Brodinsky et al., 1990) noted that 82 per cent of the mothers they interviewed concerning relinquishment expressed a desire for a reunion when their child became of age. Bouchier et al. (1991) noted that almost all the mothers in their study were hoping at some stage to resume contact with their children. Logan (1996) noted that for natural mothers, the existence of overriding feelings of guilt as a consequence of relinquishment seemed to drive their need to search.

Through the information gathered from women who gave biographical accounts of the experience of parting with their child, Wells (1994) suggests that the main reasons which emerge for natural mothers wanting to make contact is their wish to be able to explain to their child the circumstances of their birth and relinquishment. They also want an opportunity to reassure their sons or daughters that they were loved and have not been forgotten. In addition, natural mothers were often seeking reassurance from their children that their adoption was happy and a success. Wells (1994) further notes that the act of making contact would often be the first time many natural mothers felt they had control over a decision in relation to their child.

The Effects of Reunion

For natural mothers the event of adoption reunion has come about in some cases because their child has searched and in other cases because the mothers have sought contact. In all of the literature reviewed a central theme to emerge is that the event of reunion for mothers can be both a joyful and confusing period of their lives. As described earlier, despite the passage of time, in the years post-relinquishment mothers' feelings of sadness and grief often continued. When approaching reunion these feelings of guilt, self-reproach for what they had done, and worry that their child would never forgive them continued to be part of the ongoing emotional make-up of natural mothers. Little information has been provided by previous studies concerning the feelings and emotions of mothers upon being first contacted and hearing that their child was interested in contact, an event which must have been emotionally intense and traumatic. However, aspects of their emotional response to the event of the reunion meeting are referred to in a number of studies.

Taking into account the emotional response to having parted with a child, it might be expected that adoption reunion meetings would be emotionally highly charged events for natural mothers. These meetings are, by their very nature, complicated and complex events in which two people who are related by birth, but who have not been in contact since birth, come together after long periods of time have elapsed. For natural mothers, at the time of reunion, their own child, to whom they are related in the most intimate of ways, is in fact a stranger. As a result their fears and apprehensions in anticipation of a meeting are often extreme as there is no way of telling how the meeting will turn out. Cotton and Parish (1987) noted that for all the respondents in their study the reunion meetings tended to be very emotional, stressful and traumatic. McMillan and Irving (1997) found that "for most of their respondents the emotional impact of the first meeting was enormous and feelings about the experience were described by mothers in hyperbolic terms".

In relation to the outcome of reunion meetings some further common themes emerged within the literature. Whereas for some mothers the feelings of grief and sadness that they had experienced as a result of relinquishment "had lifted" (Sullivan and Groden, 1995), this was not the experience of all mothers. It appears that for some such relief was not available. Cotton and Parish (1987) noted how "issues of grief and sadness" re-emerged for all of their respondents. Their guilt about having parted with their child in the first place continued. McMillan and Irving (1997) note that for many of their respondents some aspects of the reunion process were painful. These authors instance how comments from mothers in their study demonstrated that although there are many gains for natural mothers in reunion, there was the continued awareness of what might have been, if mothers had been able to keep their children. Wells (1994) noted from autobiographical accounts which were contributed to her study that natural mothers recognised that although reunions brought happiness and joy, they also reinforced their sadness. One woman summed up the kind of feelings expressed by many natural mothers when she wrote, "we'll never, ever have what we should have had as mother and daughter . . . you can never make up or recompense what has been taken away".

A further theme to emerge from the literature in relation to post-reunion relationships was that there were in many instances problems and issues which were specific to post-reunion relationships. These problems often resulted in relationships not always being as satisfactory as mothers might have wished. The reality of adoption practice at the time of relinquishment was that when a mother parted with her child she had no control over where or with whom her child was to be raised. It might have been expected that there would be differences in social class, interests and values of the natural mothers and the parents who adopted her child. Problems arose in such instances where children were

raised in an environment that was completely different from that
of the natural mother. Slaytor (1988) found that differences in values and family life caused tensions within post-reunion relationships. Sullivan and Groden (1995) found that there were often
"feelings of incompatibility with the child due to the fact that the
child had been raised in a different culture". In a large country
such as Canada, whose population is a mix of many cultures, frus-
trations also arose post-reunion in relation to distance and the fact
that children were sometimes raised in another language. In New
Zealand, Field (1990) also found that dissatisfaction with contact
arose through issues relating to inaccessibility and difficulty in
developing feelings of closeness due to problems of distance and
as a result, infrequency of contact.

Other common issues which arose as impediments within
post-reunion relationships were jealousy between the adopted
child and children born to the mother post-adoption, and jealousy
on the part of husbands who were not the father of the adopted
child (Slaytor, 1998). Sullivan and Groden (1995) noted that their
respondents believed the reunion put a strain on their own relationships with their spouses and other children. The pain and
awkwardness of re-opening past regrets and old wounds with
family members and explaining long-held secrets was also a stress
which led to difficulties for mothers post-reunion. As a result of
these impediments, the expectations of natural mothers as to how
the relationship would develop were not always met. Despite
these disappointments however, in studies where mothers were
asked about their degree of satisfaction with relationships, more
than half of the natural mothers recorded that they were satisfied
with their relationships.[1]

Yet another common theme to emerge in all of the literature
was that mothers expressed feelings of being empowered through

[1] For instance, Slaytor (1988) records that 63 per cent of her respondents were
"completely satisfied" and 26 per cent "partly satisfied". Field (1990) found that
61 per cent of his respondents were satisfied with contact. Mullender and Kearn
(1997) report that 58 per cent of their respondents were positive about contact,
and 53 per cent had mixed reactions.

having re-established contact with their child. The renewal of contact brought an end to the years of anguish of not knowing what had happened to their child. At last, they were informed as to whether their child was alive and whether or not their adoption experience had been a happy one. The lack of control which they experienced as part of the relinquishment process was beginning to shift. Field (1990) reports that mothers recounted how their feelings of powerlessness subsided somewhat as a result of having even basic information about their child. Respondents in the study by Silverman et al. (1988) described their satisfaction and happiness through just knowing that their child was alive and well. Mothers were clear about the benefits of reunion for themselves, they described how their own self-esteem increased as a result of the healing effects of reunion (Silverman et al., 1988). As a result of simply having met their child, some mothers described themselves as being more stable emotionally (Field, 1990). For others, an improvement in self-image was a clear benefit of reunion (McMillan and Irving, 1997).

A final theme to emerge within all of the studies and biographical accounts of reunion was that, regardless of the outcome of reunions, mothers expressed how they were glad that they had gone through the experience. Whilst acknowledging the small numbers in their research, and taking account of the problems identified in relationships post-reunion, Cotton and Parish (1987) note that six of the seven mothers in their study in England were positive about having been through a reunion. In the study by Slaytor (1988) in Australia, 89 per cent of the mothers stated that they were "glad that they had gone through with a reunion". They said this whilst still identifying problems in relation to adoptive parents and problems within their own relationships with spouses. In the United States, Silverman et al. (1988) also record how 98 per cent mothers gave an extremely high satisfaction rating to their experience of reunion. In the research undertaken in Canada by Sullivan and Groden (1995), 99 per cent of the natural mothers were found to be content that they had been through a reunion. Through the meeting they had gained information about their child's life and circumstances which offered them relief and a release from the uncertainties which had left them powerless.

Overall, the research to date suggests that reunions appear to offer mothers the opportunity to reappraise and reflect on what had happened in the past. In the aftermath of meeting their child they were often able to make sense of their own feelings surrounding the adoption. Through reflecting on the forces which confronted them at the time of relinquishment, they had come to appreciate their sense of powerlessness at the time of relinquishment. In many cases, they were, as McMillan and Irving (1997) state, "able to put some ghosts to rest". The findings of all of the studies however also conclude that reunion is not the end of the story. The consequences of adoption are life long and continue above and beyond the mother and child renewing contact.

Methodological Issues

As noted earlier, the various studies on relinquishment and reunion vary from large quantitative studies, often with a qualitative element, to smaller qualitative studies. The experience of relinquishment and reunion for natural mothers from many different countries (e.g. Great Britain, Australia, New Zealand and the United States) are represented in the literature. The various studies demonstrate the strengths and limitations of different methodologies and approaches.

Recruitment

The most significant limitation noted in all of the studies reviewed was in relation to issues of recruitment. Silverman et al. (1988) suggest that "a study that involves birth parents has certain inherent difficulties because it is impossible to identify a representative sample". The vast majority of mothers, recruited for the purposes of all of the research studies, were found through the mothers having been registered with agencies which offered services in the aftermath of relinquishment or through the mother's request for reunion services. For instance, in Australia, Condon (1986) recruited 20 mothers through a natural mothers' support group. These mothers had chosen to attend the group in order to avail of the support of other mothers who had also relinquished a child. The studies undertaken by Cotton and Parish (1987) in England and by McMillan and Irving (1997) in Scotland were both undertaken within the Barnardos agency with mothers who had presented to the agency requesting counselling services. In the United States, Silverman et al. (1988) recruited their respondents through adoptee and birth-parent organisations, and a national women's magazine also carried a description of the study and an address where interested people could write for appropriate questionnaires. In four studies, Field (1990) in New Zealand, Bouchier et al. (1991) in Scotland, Sullivan and Groden (1995) in Canada and Mullender and Kearn (1997) in Great Britain), the respondents were recruited through the official adoption contact registers of the countries concerned.

All of the authors acknowledge that having recruited their sample populations through agencies which offered assistance to natural mothers, they were most likely recording the views of women who had been highly or at least sufficiently motivated to seek the assistance of an agency in the aftermath of relinquishment. One implication of this method of recruitment was that the views of mothers who have chosen not to make contact with their child are not represented. Mothers who do not know that it is possible for them to try to make contact with their child are also not represented. A further group of mothers whose views remain hidden are those women who may be too scared to contemplate contact or those who refused contact when approached on behalf of their child. Given the large numbers of women who relinquished children since the introduction of adoption,[2] it is likely

---

[2] For example, In Australia at least 250,000 women were known to have relinquished children between the late 1920s and the 1980s (Inglis, 1984, p. x); in Ireland over 40,000 women placed children for adoption between 1952 and 1999 (Adoption Board, Annual Report, 1999); in England and Wales there have been 867,355 adoption orders made since adoption was legalised in 1926 (Office of National Statistics).

that all of these groups of women make up a large proportion of the population of natural mothers. As no studies have been undertaken with this body of women, their views on relinquishment and their attitudes to a possible reunion are unknown. Limitations in relation to recruitment need therefore to be noted prior to generalisations being made in relation to all relinquishing mothers and mothers who have had a reunion.

A further limitation in the method of recruitment, which led to problems in making generalisations, was recorded by Silverman et al. (1988). Their sample, though relatively large (246), was gathered in an opportunistic rather than a systematic fashion. As a result of the questionnaire being distributed openly, it was difficult to determine how many natural parents actually received the questionnaire; thus a response rate cannot be estimated. Again, it is probable that the population of mothers who replied were those who were sufficiently motivated to want to have their views recorded.

Response Rate

A low response rate, which is often one of the limitations of postal surveys, was a factor in just one study. According to Sullivan and Groden (1995), postal surveys rarely have a response rate which exceeds 15 per cent. Slaytor (1988), whose sample population was 470 (which included adopted people and natural parents), received replies from 46 natural mothers, which was just 9 per cent of the total sample. Slaytor acknowledges the low response rate in her research. The research took place, however, when adoption reunions were just beginning to take place in Australia. The silence which had surrounded the existence of the natural mother was just starting to break. When these circumstances are taken into account the response rate may perhaps not be considered to be so low.

On the other hand, Sullivan and Groden (1995), who also undertook their survey through a postal questionnaire, had, at the beginning of their research, an expectation of a low response rate.

In their findings however, they refer to how they grossly underestimated the response rate which approached 50 per cent of those who received a survey form. For their postal survey, Mullender and Kearn (1997) also note that the response rate of 52 per cent was high. And Field (1990), who conducted a nationwide postal survey in New Zealand with a sample of 581 natural mothers, had an extremely high response rate of almost 80 per cent. In all of the studies, these high response rates were received to lengthy questionnaires which had asked for detailed responses about an extremely intimate experience. Field (1990) for example had 83 questions dealing with pregnancy and relinquishment, general psychological well-being, intensity of negative and positive feelings about adoption events and any reunion experiences. Sullivan and Groden (1995) had 34 questions which requested information from respondents on: their reasons for relinquishment, how mothers had survived in the years post-relinquishment and difficulties in relation to search and reunion. Extracting detailed responses through lengthy questionnaires did not therefore appear to be a limitation in most of the research. All of the postal surveys were, however, undertaken with women who were registered either with national contact registers or agencies who offered post-adoption services and so again were, presumably, highly motivated in relation to wanting break the silence which had surrounded the relinquishment of, and reunion with, their child.

None of the authors in any of the studies, whether postal questionnaires or qualitative interviews, remark about having had any difficulties in eliciting detailed responses about the personal experience of adoption from any the natural mothers who were surveyed. Indeed, in all studies the authors draw attention to respondents' eagerness to take part and to give detailed responses about their experience of relinquishment and reunion. Mullender and Kearn (1997) suggest that this may be attributed to the importance which natural mothers place on having their views about relinquishment and post-adoption contact placed on record despite whether they have had a reunion. According to Modell (1992), "for mothers who relinquished children for adoption, this form of narrative reconstruction can have the effect of honouring the grief of the natural mother and legitimating her desire to re-establish contact with her child" (quoted by Ochberg, 1994). In fact, therefore, it would appear that the wishes of natural mothers to have their narrative in the public arena were somewhat satisfied by being able to take part in the research studies.

Qualitative Interviews

A number of the studies on relinquishment and reunion have used qualitative interviews as part of their methodological approach. Smith (1996) suggests that qualitative research is generally concerned with exploring, understanding and describing the personal and social experiences of participants and trying to capture the meanings which particular phenomena hold for them. In one of the first studies on adoption reunion, Cotton and Parish (1987) draw attention to how, through qualitative interviews and the use of a semi-structured questionnaire, they collected comprehensive and detailed data which gave them an insight into the "sheer variety and complexity of mothers' reactions and emotions to adoption and reunion". In their discussion they acknowledge the low response rate and the consequent difficulty in drawing any general conclusions. On the other hand, they remark on how the nature of the qualitative interviews enabled them to gather comprehensive information on the unique and highly individual circumstances of each of the natural mothers. The exploration, in detail, of the mother's personal experiences gave opportunity to capture meanings which might otherwise have been missed.

When planning their research on mothers who had relinquished children, Bouchier et al. (1991) took cognisance of "the sensitive and potentially distressing nature of the interviews" and stressed that the needs of the natural mother were the main priority. As a result, their chosen methodological approach included the use of a semi-structured questionnaire which they believed gave mothers the opportunity to explore and make sense of their own experience. They also noted that they needed to allow sufficient time within the interviews for mothers to express, in their own words, their experience of relinquishment. Their method of recording involved taking extensive notes during the interviews and the authors relate how their approach enabled them to collect "vivid accounts" of the mothers' experiences. Logan (1996) also chose a qualitative approach with the use of a semi-structured questionnaire. The relinquishing mothers own detailed accounts of "their subsequent life course, and life events, including mental health" were the sensitive topics she focused on in her research. Offering women the choice of being interviewed in their own home, with periods of between 1.5 and 5 hours being given to the interview process, was believed to be a part of the methodological approach which was empowering for the women. Being sensitive to the need for privacy because of the nature and content of the interviews, and affording time and choice to women was considered to be important. In all of these studies which used qualitative interviewing techniques, the data collected appeared to be of a rich and detailed nature.

A limitation, however, which relates both to the qualitative interviews and the postal surveys, is the fact that for many of the respondents, the reporting, especially on relinquishment, was the account of an event that had taken place often 20 or more years previously. As a result memories may have been clouded by time and changing attitudes in the subsequent years. On the other hand, the fact that mothers were given the opportunity to reflect on "what might have been" and to re-examine their own role in the relinquishment and reunion experience means that what is available to us is an account of what it has been like to have lived through the event and subsequent years of having parted with a child.

Whereas most of the studies reviewed do not identity feminist principles within their methodologies, some of the features of this approach are contained in the research processes. Anderson et al. (1990) suggest that feminist research, if it is to do more than reaffirm the dominant ideologies about women and their place in the world, must begin where we are, with real, concrete people and

their actual lives. When contemplating research on the phenomenon of reunions in Australia in 1988, Slaytor records how one obvious way to start obtaining the data on how reunions had
worked "seemed to be to ask those who had already experienced
such a reunion". In her study on "Birth Mothers and their Mental
Health", Logan (1996) suggests that a feminist analysis of depression appears to be particularly relevant to understanding the outcome of relinquishment for natural mothers. In such an analysis,
relinquishment, by definition, can be seen as meaning that these
mothers were unable to live up to the socially acceptable goals of
being caring and nurturing mothers. Failure to live up to these
expectations compounded feelings of powerlessness and low self-
esteem and may render women prone to depression. For the purposes of the study undertaken by Logan (1996), it seemed reasonable therefore to approach a study on natural mothers from a
feminist perspective.

The detail which the biographical and autobiographical accounts of natural mothers add to our knowledge of the experiences of relinquishing mothers can also be viewed from a feminist
perspective. When exploring the study of feminist biography,
Reinharz (1994) states that "the history of women's lives is largely
unknown". Until the development of feminist scholarship, few
people considered the history of women to be a history at all. She
suggests that denying people a history produces socially constructed ignorance. Shulman (1984) notes that today, the feminist
biographer has a "great new audience of women hungry to know
about women" (quoted in Reinharz, 1994). The desire of mothers
to share their story so that others in the same position would have
the courage to come forth and search for their children emerges as
a central theme in all these texts (Musser, 1979; Inglis, 1984;
Wicks, 1993; Collins, 1993; Wells, 1994; Robinson, 2000). The information which these biographical accounts of relinquishing
mothers add to our knowledge of adoption and reunion assists
therefore in redressing the balance by giving recognition to their
lived experience.

The Present Study

When contemplating a study on adoption reunions in Ireland, the question as to whether the experience of reunion for Irish mothers might be similar to that of mothers in other jurisdictions was obviously of interest. Bouchier et al. (1991) report that one of the motivations for undertaking their study was that the feelings and reactions of natural mothers to the process of relinquishment which were being noted in 1984 at the Birth Link Agency, were similar to those which had been found in the Australian study by Winkler and Van Keppel (1984). Social workers in Ireland who had been facilitating search and reunion also began to observe that the feelings and reactions of natural mothers within the reunion process were similar to those which had been noted in other countries. This researcher, through her work as a professional social worker in the area of adoption reunion, noted that increasing numbers of natural mothers had begun to present themselves to the Health Board requesting a reunion service. Information relayed through discussions with other social workers practising in the field confirmed that the same phenomena were occurring throughout the country. As there was a dearth of information on the process and event of relinquishment for mothers in Ireland, and as there was no published research on reunions, it was felt that a study which would record the experiences of Irish mothers and compare their experience with mothers from other countries would be of interest.

The findings of previous studies on reunions had drawn attention to the fact that to have an insight into the process and event of relinquishment was important because it gave an insight into the frame of mind of mothers as they approached reunion. For the present study, therefore, it was deemed to be important to gather information on the issue of relinquishment and reunion. It was important to ascertain if for Irish mothers there was also a link between the emotional impact of relinquishment and its effect on mothers as they approached reunion.

Previous studies had pointed to how, for the majority of natural mothers, the event of reunion had been a cathartic event. In all studies where the question had been posed, mothers said they were happy that they had been though the reunion, and that this was the case despite whether the reunion had worked out to their satisfaction or not. Whether or not Irish mothers who had been through a reunion held the same opinion about their experience was also of interest to this research.

When contemplating the type of study to be undertaken the question as to whether the methods of enquiry which had been used in previous studies would be useful in an Irish context also arose. Through a review of the literature, it appeared that a number of the small qualitative studies and the biographical and auto-biographical accounts yielded rich and comprehensive data on natural mothers' own experience of adoption and reunion. The information gathered through semi-structured questionnaires which allowed women to tell their own story, gave vivid and very real pictures of histories that had previously been unknown. The fact that secrecy about relinquishment and adoption was the experience of Irish mothers was obvious through there being such a dearth of recorded information on the topic The strengths of qualitative interviews in enabling mothers to give their full accounts of their experience was therefore thought to be an approach which might uncover the total experiences of this group of women in Ireland. The use of direct quotations which would further enable these mothers to put their direct experience in the public discourse, appeared to be a methodological approach which would also be useful in achieving the aims of the research. The use of a feminist perspective, which reflected the researchers own values and beliefs and which had been used by Logan (1996), also appeared to be one which would enable the research to present the experience of reunion from the point of view of the mothers whose experience had not been recorded to date.

One of the gaps identified in the literature reviewed was in relation to the reactions of mothers upon being informed that their child was interested in contact. There was little information available as to what were their emotions and feelings in response to such much wanted news. How they experienced the breaking of the silence which had been their lot for so many years was un-known. It seemed possible that the range of emotions and thoughts which they had experienced would be both complex and profound. For other natural mothers and for social workers facili-tating reunions it was thought that to have information and knowledge of this period could be of assistance to other mothers contemplating reunion and so in this study it was decided to en-quire specifically about this event.

A further subject of interest about which there was only lim-ited information in previous studies was on how natural mothers perceived the development of their relationships with their chil-dren in the aftermath of reunion. How did mothers define whether a relationship was satisfactory or not, and what were the features of the relationships which made mothers satisfied or oth-erwise with the relationships. Within the present study, it was de-cided therefore to try to elicit natural mothers' opinions on the factors which they believed were influencing post-reunion rela-tionships.

In Ireland, most adoption reunions are facilitated with the as-sistance of social workers within adoption agencies. Previous studies yielded little information on whether the facilitation proc-esses and procedures used by agencies were found to be useful or beneficial to mothers involved in reunion. It was considered im-portant, therefore, to gather more information on how natural mothers experienced agency services and assistance with their reunion.

As will be seen in the following chapters, all of the foregoing issues are explored in this study.

Chapter 3

METHODOLOGY

The principal aim of this study has been to uncover the direct and personal experiences of mothers who have had a reunion with their child whom they placed for adoption.

The method of enquiry chosen for the research was a qualitative analysis of the expressed accounts of 20 mothers about their experience of adoption and reunion. The data and information were collected through in-depth, one-to-one interviews with a sample of mothers who had been through such a reunion. These interviews gave the women involved the opportunity to provide their own narrative of their experience.

Additional information was sought through written and telephone enquiries with the Adoption Board and six adoption agencies. The purpose of these enquiries was to establish when the Adoption Board and adoption agencies began to receive a significant number of search and tracing requests.[1] The general response was that a noticeable number of requests for tracing and search began to be made of the agencies from the early 1990s and some specifically mentioned 1993 and 1994. Some of these agencies have kept statistics on the numbers of requests received and the number of reunions facilitated and some have not. There are,

---

[1] The Adoption Board and the Adoption Agencies all commented that they received a very small number of requests over the years from 1960 to 1994. In general, these requests were not acted upon, with the enquirer being informed that the system of closed adoption precluded the agency from making contact with the other party.

however, no statistics compiled nationally in relation to the over-all numbers of people involved in search and reunion.

Feminist Research

Lentin (1993) views as feminist that research which tries to develop theories that explain the world from women's point of view and conceptualises reality so as to reflect women's interests and values. McCarl Neilson (1990) describes feminist research as contextual, inclusive, experiential, socially relevant and inclusive of emotions and events as experienced. She says that "to consciously adopt a woman's perspective means to see things one did not see before and also to see the familiar rather differently". Lentin (1993) quotes Shields and Dervin's (1993) summary of four elements that methodologies in feminist research have striven to incorporate:

- Women's experience of their social and personal world: feminist research treats women's experience as a scientific resource, it is actor-centred.

- The pervasive influence of gender and gender relations as social constructions.

- Reflexivity on the part of the researcher so that she is conscious of how her values, attitudes and perceptions are influencing the research process and her interaction with the interviewees.

- The emancipation of women through providing them with the information gathered in the research process.

Cook and Fonow (1990) also suggest that feminist methodology involves a concern with notions of feminist consciousness, and that by its nature it is consciousness-raising. They say that in creating an understanding of what has been previously taken for granted, in identifying the mundane aspects of social reality, the factors that oppress women and reinforce male domination become evident. As a consequence, feminist research can have a consciousness-raising effect on the subjects and on the researcher herself. In favouring feminist methodologies as a means of recording women's experience McCarl Neilson (1990) suggests that the strength of feminist methodology is that it does not deny or discount the subjective, but rather seeks to validate the private, emotional, interiorised and intimate world of women. As one of the principal aims of this study was to uncover the intimate experiences of mothers in relation to adoption and reunion from the mothers' own perspectives, the use of feminist methodology was considered to be appropriate.

Qualitative Research

Glesne and Peshkin (1992) maintain that qualitative research seeks to make sense of personal stories and the ways in which the stories of the respondents in the research intersect with each other. Qualitative research deals with multiple, socially constructed variables that are complex, and so it regards the research task as coming to understand and interpret how the various participants in a social setting construct and interpret the world around them. Miles and Huberman (1994) state that qualitative data are a source of well-grounded, rich descriptions and explanations of processes in identifiable local contexts. They claim that words, organised into incidents or stories about human relationships, have a concrete, vivid, meaningful flavour. It is their contention that human relationships have peculiarities which make the understanding of them more complex, and that it is also necessary to contend with the influences of institutions, structures, practices and conventions that people reproduce and transform. They further contend that human meanings and intentions are worked out within the frameworks of these social structures, structures that are often invisible but nonetheless real.

Norris (1997) suggests that qualitative methods give us a way to write about the lives of our participants in context and to provide for our audience the surprise of a recognizable person. Marshall and Rossman (1995) suggest that a qualitative approach means that the participant's perspective is sought directly, recorded and analysed. The starting point, as Hill et al. (1999) suggest, is the idea that reality is socially constructed rather than objectively determined.

Miles and Huberman (1994) state that the strength of qualitative data is that it allows a strong handle on "real-life" situations, situations that have occurred in ordinary life and in natural settings. Furthermore, with regard to data collected through qualitative research, they state that:

> Confidence is buttressed by local groundedness, i.e. the fact that the data are collected in close proximity to a specific situation. The influences of the local context are not stripped away but are taken into account and the possibility for understanding latent, underlying or non-obvious issues is strong. Qualitative data, with their emphasis on people's lived experience are fundamentally well suited for locating the meanings people place on events, processes and structures in their lives and for connecting these meanings to the social worlds around them.

Mahon, Conlon and Dillon (1998) in their recent study on the sensitive topic of crisis pregnancy discuss why they chose to use qualitative in-depth interviews when interviewing the women for their study. They refer to the concerns of feminist research which point to women's unequal position in social, political and academic spheres. They say that qualitative, one-to-one, in-depth interviews have been a key component in feminist research as they are seen as a way of collecting data which is capable of centralising the women's own experiences, being responsive to the respondent, being flexible and reflective and negotiating the power relations between the researcher and the researched.

In order to uncover and reach an understanding of the mothers' experiences of adoption and reunion, good qualitative data of the nature described above and from which meaningful interpretations could be made were required for this study. In an effort, therefore, to ensure that this type of information and data was elicited, a qualitative approach was the chosen method of obtaining information.

Justifying the Research

Rubin and Rubin (1995) state that in the beginning of the research almost anyone in the arena knows enough to be able to help the research and that as the research progresses it is necessary to talk to people who have particular knowledge to help you test specific themes.

In order to establish whether there was interest and support for research about adoption reunions, the researcher spoke with ten social workers involved in the field. These social workers were identified through the Council of Irish Adoption Agencies which represents all adoption agencies. The social workers with whom the researcher consulted had been facilitating adoption reunions for periods of up to ten years as a part of their general adoption practice. They were familiar with research which had been carried out in other countries and were interested to establish if the findings of a research study in Ireland would have similar results. They were aware that there had been no research to date on adoption reunions in Ireland, and all said they thought there was a need to have research data available for the purpose of informing social work practice and to campaign for change in adoption legislation. They also indicated that their agencies would be interested in facilitating the research by requesting mothers with whom they worked to take part in the research. In was their opinion that many of these mothers would want to share their experience with others by participating in a research project as had been the situation in previous research in other countries.

Four mothers, known to the researcher through her own work as a professional social worker, were also consulted on the question of the usefulness of the research. Two of these mothers had been through a reunion and two had plans to try to do so when their child reached the age of eighteen. All of them said they thought it was essential to record the history and details of their experiences as mothers who had to part with their children. They also thought that it would be useful for mothers contemplating a reunion to know what the experience of women in the same situations had been.

Two experienced researchers, at two separate academic institutions, were also consulted to enquire if they thought that the subject was worthy of study. Both were strongly supportive and pointed to the lack of research in Ireland on adoption reunions and suggested that it was a subject worth researching.

Selection of Agencies

In Ireland in 1998 there were 15 adoption agencies registered with the Adoption Board. All of these agencies offered tracing and reunion services to mothers who placed their children for adoption. There was also one organisation which offered a professional tracing and reunion service but which was not a registered adoption agency. These agencies, because they had been facilitating adoption reunions for some time, were considered likely to have a population of mothers who had been through a reunion. Due to the sensitive nature of the subject, and in some cases the secrecy which still exists about adoption, it was thought that an approach to mothers through their agency social worker would be the most successful way of recruiting a sample of mothers who had been through a reunion. As outlined in the literature review, previous studies (Silverman, 1988; Slaytor, 1988; Field, 1990; Sullivan, 1995; Mullender and Kearn, 1997) had inherent difficulties in recruiting a representative sample of all natural mothers and it was thought that comparable factors in relation to the intimate and often secret nature of relinquishment might be the situation in Ireland. The limited time and resources available to the researcher were also taken into account when deciding on the method of recruitment.

Five agencies were chosen to give a geographical spread of agencies throughout Ireland, both north and south. They were also chosen in order to represent a mix of voluntary adoption agencies and Health Board (statutory) adoption agencies.

Before selecting the agencies for inclusion in the research, a set of criteria were drawn up so as to ensure that a representative sample of mothers could be reached. Within its client population each agency was required to have:

- Mix of urban and rural

- Mix of different religious denominations

- Mix of social class

- Mix of age range.

The agency also had to:

- Be operating search and reunion services for at least five years

- Be able to access four mothers who were at least one year post-reunion

- Be staffed by professionally qualified social workers

- Be interested and willing to take part in the research.

All the agencies chosen met the above criteria. It was thought that a representative cross-section of mothers could be found through interviews with clients of the five chosen agencies. The selection process does not claim to be representative in a statistical sense. What was more important for the selection procedure to provide to the research process was:

- A sufficient number of women who had experienced a reunion in order to undertake a research study

- A population of women who were at least one year post-reunion

- A population of women who were willing to speak about the experience

- A number of women who were able to give a full narrative account of what a reunion had been like for them as the mother of a child who had been adopted.

Numbers to be Interviewed

Each agency was asked to identify four women who had been through a reunion with their child. As this was a limited qualitative study of the women's direct experience of adoption and reunion, it was thought that twenty interviews would give ample information and insight into the experience of adoption and reunion. The time and resources available to the researcher to undertake the study were also influencing factors in choosing 20 women.

Identifying Respondents through the Agencies

Marshall and Rossman (1995) say that it is essential to convince the agencies from whom the researcher requires assistance that the research is substantive, will contribute to the field, is well conceived and that the researcher is capable of conducting the research. The agencies were aware that the researcher was a professionally qualified social worker with a knowledge and understanding of the sensitivity of adoption and reunion. The need for strict confidentiality was also understood and guaranteed. The agencies were also informed that the research was being conducted through a recognised academic institution and that the standards required by the institution would be adhered to throughout the research process.

Formal Request to Agencies

Between January and March 1998, a letter officially inviting each of the five agencies to take part in the research was sent to the Senior Social Worker in each agency (Appendix 1). The letter gave details of the aims and purpose of the research, details of how it was proposed to carry out the fieldwork and how it was proposed to interview respondents.

How the Agencies Identified the Respondents

The social workers within the agencies contacted the mothers by phone, through a group, via letters or at an interview session. The social workers justified their differing approaches on the basis of how they thought the purpose of the research could be most clearly explained to their client. Given the sensitive nature of the information being sought the social workers wished to explain how any information shared would be used. All of the women who were approached subsequently stated that they were satisfied with the way they were asked to participate.

When the women agreed to take part, they gave permission for their names and addresses to be forwarded to the researcher and further contact was to be made directly between the mother and the researcher. At this point the agency's involvement in the research ceased. In all, 20 women were approached by five agencies, four women per agency. Eighteen (90 per cent) of these women agreed to take part in the research. Two women (10 per cent) declined to participate.

Undertaking the Research

Semi-structured Interviews

The nature of the information requested from the women in this study consisted of detailed accounts of how they had experienced adoption and reunion. It was important therefore to choose an approach to interviewing which would elicit the best possible information and detail. The use of an Interview Guide (Appendix 3) which contained a series of semi-structured questions was chosen as the most expedient to obtain the information required. Robson (1993) says that the semi-structured interview is one where the interviewer has worked out the questions in advance, but is free to modify thereafter based on her perception of what seems most appropriate in the context of the conversation. Patton (1990) describes the interview guide as a list of questions or issues that are to be explored in the course of the interview. An interview guide is prepared in order to ensure that basically the same information is obtained from all the respondents. The interview guide provides topics within which the interviewer is free to explore, probe, and ask questions that will elucidate and illuminate that particular subject. The interview guide helps make interviewing across a number of different respondents more systematic and comprehensive by delimiting in advance the issues to be explored.

Patton (1990) suggests that probes can be used as a further tool to guide the interview so that the information required is obtained. He suggests that probes should be used to deepen a response to the question and to increase the richness of the data being obtained. Robson (1993) says that a probe is a device available to the interviewer to encourage the interviewee to expand on information given. In the present study, probes were used where necessary both to deepen and increase the amount of information and to give cues to the respondents about the level of response desired.

The Pilot Interviews

Robson (1993) state that there is no complete substitute for a pilot study as it involves the researcher in the "real" situation prior to the final research interviews. It enables the researcher to decide whether what is proposed is feasible in terms of time, effort and resources. It also gives the researcher the opportunity to refine the interview guide and the data collection plan. Glesne and Peshkin (1992) say that ideally pilot study participants should be drawn from the target population.

For the present study, two mothers known to the researcher through her work agreed to take part in a pilot interview. They were not part of the final study. Both of these women had met with their child over a year prior to the pilot interview. The study, along with its aims and purpose, were explained to them. They said they were interested to take part in order to share their own experience of reunion and said that they would have appreciated knowing about other mothers' experiences before they undertook their own reunion.

Experience and information gathered through the pilot study pointed to the fact that if at all possible it was essential to have a completely private space for interview. One of the pilot interviews was conducted in a hotel lobby (at the interviewee's request) and the other in the interviewee's home. The nature of the questions was extremely personal and often triggered sad memories for the women involved. It was therefore noted that a private space to cry and express grief was important.

Subsequent to the pilot interviews, as a result of the manner in which respondents approached the telling of their story, the semi-structured questions on the interview guide were refined. It was apparent that the respondents wished to give details of the relinquishment in order to give the whole story of adoption. The focus of this research however was reunion, and so it was decided that the sequence of questioning would be to ask firstly about the reunion. The need to ask for more details with regard to age of respondents, dates of birth of the children who had been adopted and geographical location was also noted. The advantage of recording the interviews on tape became clear as one of the pilot interviews was taped and handwritten notes were taken of the other. The taped interview yielded much richer and more detailed information on the experience of the women involved.

The Fieldwork

As stated, 18 (90 per cent) of the women approached by the agencies agreed to take part in the research. It is worth noting the reasons in one case, and the process in the other, which led to two women choosing not to take part.

Non-respondents

Two women chose not to take part in the research. One had been contacted by an agency social worker initially by phone, and agreed over the phone that the letter of introduction explaining the research be sent to her by the agency. The letter was duly sent and when no response had been received after two months, the social worker involved was asked by the researcher to contact the woman again. When no response was received after a total period of four months the social worker wrote to the researcher stating what had been done and how the agency was of the opinion that the woman in question was choosing not to take part.

The other woman was contacted initially through a letter from her social worker. The woman rang the social worker directly, declining the invitation to take part. She said that she wished to give her reasons for not agreeing to be interviewed. She told the social worker that her reunion had not worked out according to her hopes and wishes. She was in fact no longer in contact with her child. She stated that she found it too painful to talk about the whole process and as a result did not feel she wanted to be part of the research.

The need to approach the potential respondents with extreme sensitivity was an issue with which the researcher was familiar through her experience in adoption work. The experience of this potential respondent was that despite efforts to approach her in a sensitive way, the issue of parting with a child was too painful for her to share for research purposes.

Contacting the Women Who Agreed to Take Part

In order to organise the interviews the researcher phoned each of the women in order to agree a date, time and place that was convenient for the potential respondents and also to allow for some efficiency in travelling time for the researcher. The researcher informed each respondent that she was willing to travel, in all cases, to the town where the respondent now lived and to interview her at a location of her choice. The first choice, for perceived reasons of privacy, was the home of the respondent. Eleven mothers chose to be interviewed at home. The other nine chose an office or other location which was identified by the researcher.

Agreeing to a location where the respondents said they would be most comfortable was important since the mothers were being asked to describe a very intimate and personal experience to a stranger. It was also important that the mothers were able to partake in decisions about how they would be involved.

The Interview Guide

The first questions on the interview guide (Appendix 3) took details of name, age, address, year of placing child for adoption, date of birth of child and where the adopted adult now lived. The remainder of the questions were explorative and sought to gather information on the following:

1. How did the mother make a decision to contact or to respond to contact from her child?

2. How was the contact made?

3. What were the mother's feelings in relation to being contacted?

4. What was the reunion like?

5. What were the mother's feelings and thoughts about the reunion?

6. How had things developed since the reunion?

7. What were the mother's recollections of the pregnancy and placing her child for adoption?

8. How did the mother experience the service of the agency that facilitated the reunion?

In drawing up these topics for the interview guide account was taken of the findings of previous research studies in other countries (Condon, 1986; Cotton and Parish, 1987; Bouchier, 1991; Sullivan, 1995). This was done in order to confirm or refute their applicability to the experience of Irish women.

Conducting the Interviews

All of the interviews took place between August and December of 1998.

Robson (1993) suggests that when carrying out an enquiry in-
volving human beings we should take advantage of the fact that
they can tell us things about themselves during a conversation or
within an interview. He cites Cannel and Kahan as saying that a
conversation is an interview when it is one "initiated by the interviewer for the specific purpose of obtaining research relevant information and focused by him on content specified by research
objectives of systematic description, prediction or explanation".
Marshall and Rossman (1995) describe in-depth interviewing as a
data collection method which is relied on quite extensively by
qualitative researchers and again cite Cannel and Kahn as saying
that an in-depth interview is "a conversation with a purpose". The
researcher explores a few general topics to help uncover the participants' interpretation of the meaning of what has happened for
them, but otherwise respects how the participant frames and
structures the responses. This in fact is an assumption fundamental to qualitative research — the participants' perspective on the
phenomenon of interest should unfold as the participant views it,
not as the researcher views it.

Robson (1993) says that to make profitable use of this flexibility,
considerable skill and experience are called for from the interviewer. The researcher in this instance brought the experience of 15
years in professional social work and 5 years in adoption, much of
which was specifically with mothers and adopted adults involved
in search and reunion. When discussing research on sensitive topics, Lee (1993) suggests that areas of personal experience, such as
bereavement, can be emotionally charged. Adoption and adoption
reunion, as part of their inherent structure and process, are built on
loss. Experience and knowledge of the area and the possible effect
that the interview processes may have had on the women who
were to take part in this study were strengths brought to the research by the training and experience of the researcher.

The researcher met each of the mothers in their chosen location. The use of the interview guide as well as the purpose of the
semi-structured nature of the interviews was explained to them.
They were informed that interviews would take about 90 minutes.

In fact, five interviews continued for up to two hours as the mothers' responses contained great detail about their experiences.

The researcher's wish to record the interviews on tape and the reasons for wanting to do so were explained to the participants. How the tapes would be transcribed at home by the researcher, and how their account would not be divulged to any other person except her academic supervisor at the university until all identifying names and dates were removed, was also explained. They were informed that the tapes would then be kept in a safe place until the research was completed, at which time they would be destroyed or returned to the respondents if they so wished. Five respondents said they felt awkward about being taped but were willing to go ahead. One woman was more cautious and asked that the tape be returned to her immediately upon transcription. It was explained to this respondent that the tape might be needed in order to check facts from the script at a later date. The respondent offered assurance that the tape would be kept safely at her home, with the researcher having access to it at any time.

All the respondents were offered a copy of the transcript once it was completed. They were informed, however, that the interviews and information as given at the time of interview would be the information used for the research and that by supplying them with a copy of the script, the interviewer was not offering a chance to change information supplied, apart from details with regard to dates. Half of the respondents requested a copy of their script. In the event, no respondent contacted the researcher to offer corrections. All the respondents were informed that they would be contacted when the research was complete and that a copy of the final text would be made available to them to read if they so wished.

In explaining the aims and purpose of the study, and the nature of feminist qualitative research, the researcher outlined how she wished to use direct quotes from the interviews in order to give a true account of the women's experiences of search and reunion. Rubin and Rubin (1995) say that asking for permission to use specific quotes indicates that you think the answers are worthy of quoting and shows that you respect the interviewees' ownership of their words. All of the respondents were agreeable to direct quotations from their interviews being used.

When the interviews were completed and the tapes transcribed, the researcher wrote to the respondents to thank them for their participation. During the six months following the interviews the researcher was approached by three social workers who had been working with the informants asking about the results of the research and when it would be completed. For this reason, during the period of the writing up the research, the interviewer wrote again to each respondent to tell them of the progress of the research and to assure them that they would have access to the results and findings when it was completed.

Lentin and Byrne (2000) say that "feminist methodology gives us permission to be explicit about the problems we encounter as we seek to reduce the possibility of further exploitation in our research relationships with other human beings". The attention to details such as place of interview, how the interviews were conducted and how information provided would be used was important in ensuring that the mothers involved were given input into the research process and that they did not feel exploited.

Conducting the interviews was a challenging experience. It was essential to be able to create an atmosphere where participants felt comfortable enough to discuss their experience of relinquishment and reunion. Through the creation of an empathetic atmosphere within the interview the women chose to trust the researcher and reveal their innermost feelings about adoption and reunion. The women were eager to talk and tell their stories but they were often extremely upset and emotional in relation to the loss they had experienced. Sixteen of the eighteen mothers became visibly upset and cried during interview. An ability to be sensitive to the depth of feelings and intensity of grief felt by them was an essential component in being able to continue the interviews and guide the women through to the end. The skills acquired over the past 15 years as a social work practitioner proved to be important.

As part of the introduction process the women had been informed that I was a practising social worker in the area of adoption and reunion. The purpose of relaying this information was to inform them that I had previous knowledge and experience in the area of adoption and reunion. I believed that this might make it easier for them to talk with me during the interviews. The respondents had all had their reunions facilitated through a social worker and many had ongoing contact with a social work service. The need to clarify the differences in my role of researcher as opposed to that of a social work practitioner within the interview process was therefore essential at the beginning of the interview. This was done in order to bring some objectivity to the study and to ensure that boundaries were established to enable the data to be collected in a coherent and consistent fashion.

When discussing the use of a feminist perspective in interviewing women, however, Oakley (1981, quoted in McCarl Neilson, 1990) points to how taking textbook advice about interviewing (for example, to maintain a certain distance between yourself and the interviewee or to avoid answering questions) not only would not work but would also limit her ability to communicate with respondents in a way that would generate worthwhile and meaningful information. Her approach, therefore, included answering questions which the women in her study posed during the interviews. This approach proved to be a successful strategy in eliciting the information required and easing the anxieties of the respondents during the interview process. The benefits which might accrue through adopting the same approach in this study were considered prior to interview and it was decided that questions which were asked of me during the interviews would be answered to the best of my knowledge.

Analysis of Data

Data analysis is the process of bringing order, structure and meaning to the mass of data collected through the interview process which may have relevance to the research study. The analysis of qualitative data collected through the interview process involves a search for general statements about relationships among categories of data in order to identify common themes (Marshall and Rossman, 1995). Central to the methodological approach of this study was the use of feminist research methods which included the requirement to be self-reflexive within the research process. Thus, once the interviews had been completed, in order to organise and select material for the analysis, I initially found it useful to engage directly with the data by personally transcribing the taped interviews. Undertaking this task afforded a further opportunity to engage and become familiar with the verbal accounts of the mothers and so provided further insights into their emotional reactions to the experience of relinquishment and reunion. It also afforded an opportunity to take cognisance of how the questions posed in the interviews had been received, to reflect on how the objectives of the research actually were achieved through the process of qualitative interviewing, and to search for biases which may have been present throughout the process. Self-reflexivity, according to Lentin (1993), is an essential part of feminist research. We are what we study; the reflection upon acknowledgement of one's own objectives and biases therefore become part of the research findings.

Once interview scripts have been transcribed, the category generation phase of data analysis begins. This process of category generation involves noting regularities and irregularities within and between the accounts of the participants. According to Marshall and Rossman (1995), it is important that the categories be internally consistent but distinct from one another. Within feminist qualitative research what the researcher is seeking to identify are the salient, grounded categories of meaning held by the participants in the setting. Mothers who had been interviewed for this research had all been through a reunion with their child who had been adopted and the aim of this study was to seek information on what this particular experience had been like for them. From each of the detailed narrative scripts, therefore, direct quotations from mothers which appeared to represent these respondents' own definitions of their experience of reunion were identified and highlighted. Within the interviews mothers had also been asked to give detailed accounts of their experience of the period leading up to reunion. They were further asked to give their reflections on the reunion meeting and an account of how they perceived the subsequent relationship in the aftermath of reunion. Direct quotations which gave a picture of their personal and emotional experience of relinquishment and of how adoption impacted on their lives were therefore also identified. The use of these quotations meant that the direct accounts of the mothers were the basis of analysis which was an important element of the feminist research principles of this study. Once the salient quotes had been identified, through the use of charts and tables, the emerging themes and patterns were then categorised, noting common experiences and regularities from the scripts.

Lincoln and Guba (1985, quoted in Robson, 1993) suggest that there are a number of questions which must be addressed in relation to credibility in any systematic enquiry of human beings. Firstly, they suggest that it is essential to ascertain the "truth value" of the information obtained in order to establish confidence in the data collected. Secondly, questions in relation to the "applicability" of the findings to another setting or group of people need to be posed. The need for "consistency" in the data collection and analysis needs to be examined in order that one can have confidence that the findings would be replicated if the study were repeated. Finally, Lincoln and Guba (1985) say that questions need to be posed in relation to "neutrality" which is called for in the research process in order to be sure that the findings are determined by the respondents and in context, and not only by the biases, motivations, interests or perspectives of the enquirer.

Robson (1993) suggests that to enhance credibility within the analysis it is important to demonstrate that the subject of the enquiry was accurately identified and described. For purposes of this study, as outlined earlier, in order to ensure accurate identification of mothers who had been through a reunion, the potential respondents were identified through agencies whose work entailed the facilitation of reunions and who in particular had offered services to the potential respondents. Robson (1993) further suggests that within the research process "prolonged involvement and persistent observation enhances credibility". The knowledge gained through prolonged involvement can build trust and ensure familiarity on the part of the researcher with the topic under investigation. Through my work as a professional social worker in adoption in the years prior to the research project I had gained a lot of information and knowledge through facilitating adoption reunions which was invaluable in the search for common themes, subjects and ideas when analysing the data.

When undertaking the analysis of qualitative data it is also important to address the issue of the transferability of potential findings to other, possibly similar, situations. Within this study the small number of respondents in the sample does not permit meaningful classification in a statistical sense and therefore the study cannot claim to be statistically representative. Neither, as a result of the small numbers interviewed, can the same kind of generalisations be made as might have been done with a larger population and a more representative sample of natural mothers. Rather the presentation of a sample of the narratives of natural mothers in relation to their own personal experience of reunion provides a detailed and vivid account of the history of relinquishment and reunion. The comprehensive and detailed accounts of these mothers give a rich and deep insight into the actual lived experience of reunion of these women who have been at the heart of adoption and reunion. Through the presentation of such detailed information Lincoln and Guba (quoted in Robson, 1993) suggest that transferability judgements may be made as a result, for instance, of being totally familiar with the similarity between one case and a second. One of the purposes in using the direct narrative accounts of relinquishment and reunion of these mothers is therefore to add to the credibility and dependability of the data presented.

When discussing the issue of "confirmability" of the findings of a research study, Robson (1993) outlines how a detailed description of the research methodology can provide what he terms as an "audit trail" which can be used to assess the confirmability of a study's findings. Such an audit trail of the processes involved in deciding on a feminist qualitative approach for this study were described earlier in this section. Details of the methods used in the recruitment of participants and the conduct of qualitative interviews were also outlined. The method of recording the interviews was described, and reference made to the fact that respondents were offered the opportunity to have a copy of the transcription of the interview if they so wished. This process was deemed to be important as part of the feminist research approach which demands that through the reciprocal sharing of knowing between researchers and researched, those researched become collaborators in the research project (Lentin, 1993).

In relation to the analysis of the findings, at the time of interview the permission of the respondents had been sought to use their direct quotations from their narrative accounts. It had been explained to them that the aim of this research was to present the experience of reunion from the direct perspective of natural mothers. Questions such as, "Tell me about the decision to search", "About the period leading up to reunion", "How is the relationship going now", and "What factors are influencing the relationship" were specifically posed in an open-ended way so that mothers could relate details about their own personal situation and how it had developed for them. Whereas the answers were given in the form of a free-flowing account, all of the respondents used the opportunity to relate and identify the factors which were particular to their own experience of reunion and relinquishment. When analysing the data therefore, choosing the issues and themes which were common and of consequence to the reunion process was done through extracting quotations which gave the mothers' own perception of what, for instance, were the important factors influencing the post-reunion relationship, or what was the emotional experience of the period from initial contact to reunion.

The rationale for the sequence in which the findings of this research are presented emerged during the initial stages of the analysis of the data. Despite the fact that the primary aim of this research was to present an account of the experience of reunion from the

perspective of natural mothers, the findings are presented in a sequence which starts with a description of the event of crisis pregnancy and moves on to giving detailed accounts of the process and
consequences of relinquishment. Following this are the mothers'
accounts of the experience of contact being made with their child
and then descriptions of the reunion meetings. The final section is
devoted to post-reunion issues such as the establishment of relationships and the effects of reunion on the natural mothers.

During the process of analysing the data from the narratives of
the natural mothers, it became clear to the researcher that the process of relinquishment could not be separated from the event of reunion. When mothers were answering questions in relation to reunion and describing the process of reunion from their point of
view they often referred back to the circumstances and pain of relinquishment. In fact, in the majority of scripts the accounts of relinquishment and the effect of adoption on the lives of the mothers
are longer and more detailed than the accounts and details of reunion. The need which the respondents appeared to have to place the
reunion in context was an essential part of the telling of their story.
The use of a feminist methodological approach which, as described
by McCarl Neilson (1990), allows for the context to be described
and the inclusion of the emotions of events as they were experienced enabled the interviews therefore to proceed as the mothers
believed to be important. The importance of asking the question,
"Does this work for women?", which McCarl Neilson (1990) suggests as integral to feminist scholarship in relation to the analysis of
the data, was demonstrated. It made sense therefore to present the
findings which are outlined in the following chapters within the
contexts defined by the mothers who were interviewed.

Chapter 4

PREGNANCY AND RELINQUISHMENT

"When I think of it, an animal would fight for its child but I didn't. I just did what I was told to do, and I thanked them for it." (Res 1)

In a comprehensive study on crisis pregnancy, Mahon (1998) outlines how, even in the late 1990s, the reaction of many unmarried women to a crisis pregnancy was one of shock. Traditionally in Ireland there has been a high degree of stigma attached to being an unmarried mother. Being single and pregnant still carries a degree of stigma. The prospect of lone motherhood is a stereotypically stigmatised social identity (Mahon, 1998).

This chapter looks at the reactions of the mothers to the crisis they experienced upon discovering they were pregnant. The majority (14) of these pregnancies occurred during the 1970s. The remainder occurred in the 1960s and 1950s. Reactions and levels of support offered to the pregnant women by their families and by the putative fathers are described, including the women's experience of the measures taken by parents to hide and ensure secrecy around the pregnancy. Descriptions of how a decision to part with their child was arrived at are given from the mothers' perspective. The impact of the silencing of their motherhood in the aftermath of relinquishment and the grief experienced in the following years are recounted. Finally, the efforts of the mothers who tried to regain some control by keeping in touch with their child through the agencies are given, as are the experiences of the mothers for whom this was not an option.

The age of the respondents at the time of birth ranged from 16 to 31. Of the total 18, 16 were 22 years or under.

Table 4.1: Age of Respondents at Time of Birth of Child

Number of Mothers	Age at Birth of Child
2	16
3	17
1	18
3	20
3	21
4	22
1	24
1	31
Total 18	

At the time of pregnancy with their child, the majority of the respondents were employed. Seven respondents were employed in the service/hospitality industry, six were employed in office work and two were employed in factory work. Two respondents were third level students and one respondent was at school. The social class of the respondents was therefore spread across a wide range.

Reaction to Crisis Pregnancy

Respondents' Reaction

All of the respondents described being shocked and upset when their pregnancy was confirmed.

> *"It was just heavy petting or whatever that is, so it was totally a shock." (Res 9)*

Some respondents said they were so innocent at the time that they wondered how it could have happened.

> *"I hadn't a clue, it could have gone into my ear and I wouldn't have known, and at the doctor's I didn't know what positive meant." (Res 18)*

Others said they were scared and they were not sure whom they could tell:

> *"I was terrified, on my own, could tell no one." (Res 2)*

> *"I was getting sicker and sicker every morning and trying to hide that from the girls in the flat." (Res 17)*

There seemed to be nowhere to turn, and they were not sure where they would get help:

> *"I was very upset, I didn't know what to do, hadn't a clue what I was going to do." (Res 17)*

For one respondent the shock reaction led to her wanting to deny the pregnancy:

> *"And not knowing what to do, thinking the thing was going to go away." (Res 9)*

Despite being in shock, in denial or overwhelmed with panic, all of these young women knew they were "in trouble" and that they would eventually have to face the consequences. None of the respondents were able to say that they felt happy to be pregnant. The prospect of lone motherhood was perceived as a crisis.

Once they suspected or had confirmed their pregnancy, twelve of the eighteen respondents told their parents, two told siblings only, two confided in friends and two told only their boyfriends.

Table 4.2: Who Was Told about Pregnancy

Who Was Told	Number
Parents	12
Siblings	2
Friends	2
Boyfriend	2
TOTAL	18

In terms of to whom information about the pregnancy was disclosed no particular pattern (e.g. urban/rural, age at conception or year of conception) could be discerned across the respondents.

Parental and Family Reaction to Pregnancy

The twelve respondents who told their parents were either living at home or visiting every weekend and they knew that the physical evidence of their pregnancy would soon become evident. This frequency of contact suggests that they were well integrated into their families. Those who told siblings or friends chose to do so because they felt their parents would be either angry or upset. The parents of the two respondents who told only their boyfriends were deceased, and they chose not to tell siblings for fear that they would be angry or distressed.

Six respondents reported that they were offered some support when they announced that they were pregnant. The support offered, however, was not sufficient to enable them to feel secure enough to consider keeping their child.

In one instance siblings were supportive, but this depended on parents not being told. In two instances, where respondents stated that their boyfriends had been supportive their families were not, and so it was not possible for them to think about keeping their child.

The twelve respondents who told their families all recounted how their parents were extremely upset at the news:

> *"My father was awful upset, very upset, my mother was in a state of shock." (Res 12)*

The news created conflict within families about how the young woman should be supported.

Two respondents stated that their parents were abusive, both physically and verbally.

> *"Daddy called me every name under the sun and the other kids were sitting around wondering . . ." (Res 14)*

> *"My mother found out and she hit me and thumped me and called me all the names under the sun." (Res 17)*

One respondent recounted how she felt her mother supported her, but her father was damning:

> *"My mother was cool out, she was brilliant. . . . My father, he said 'we'll send you to England and get rid of it, or you are out of here'." (Res 18)*

One respondent stated that her sibling was supportive but there were conditions attached:

> *"I told my sister, she was six years older than me but she said not to open my mouth to my parents." (Res 16)*

Respondent 11 also said that during her pregnancy her siblings were supportive but it was dependent on her obtaining employment outside the country so that she had an excuse not to visit her mother and therefore not inform her of her pregnancy. Her siblings colluded in a web of secrecy about her pregnancy which ensured that her mother and people in the locality from which she came would never know that she was unmarried and pregnant.

During the interviews the respondents found it extremely difficult and upsetting to recount the reactions of their parents and also the lack of support they felt they had experienced. Many were visibly upset and cried as they gave their accounts. It seemed to the respondents that when they were at their most vulnerable and when they needed the help and support of their families, for most it was not forthcoming.

Putative Father's Reaction to Pregnancy

Thirteen respondents turned to the putative father for support. The nature and length of time of the relationship between putative fathers and the respondents varied considerably. In some cases it was a short-lived, apparently casual contact, in other cases a serious relationship of as long as three years' duration preceded the pregnancy. Consequently the responses varied:

- Four of the respondents were offered support from the putative father.

- Nine respondents told their boyfriends, but they either severed contact or did not offer realistic support.

- Five of the respondents said that they chose not to inform their boyfriends that they were expecting a child.

(a) Putative father supportive. Four respondents described being offered support by the putative fathers. For two of the respondents the support of their boyfriends was available to them throughout the pregnancy. When one of the respondents left the country to have her child her boyfriend kept in touch and helped her financially. Commenting on this she said:

> *"And he couldn't come over to see me because then everyone would know. At that time a girlfriend and boyfriend didn't go on holidays together, everything was totally different, but he used to send me money to the post office." (Res 5)*

However, while she felt supported by the putative father of her child, this support was inadequately articulated. Consequently, she felt that she was left with the emotional burden of the pregnancy:

> *"We didn't talk about it really, and whenever I wanted to talk he would just say, 'don't be worrying yourself, it will be all right'." (Res 5)*

In the other case (Respondent 14), the putative father was supportive throughout pregnancy and also during the adoption process. Parental pressure on both the respondent and her boyfriend was cited as the reason for the child having been relinquished.

Both of these respondents ultimately married the fathers of their children. Given the social mores of the time, it was impossible for them to countenance keeping their child in the context of a non-marital relationship. As a result the children were lost to them.

For the other two respondents who described the putative father as supportive, the support offered was ultimately rejected by the respondents themselves. In both of these cases the women made a moral choice to assume full responsibility for the pregnancy because they were not comfortable with the nature of the relationship with the putative father.

In the case of one of these respondents, the boyfriend had taken charge of the situation by having the pregnancy test done and informing the respondent's parents of the pregnancy. But when this respondent refused to marry her boyfriend his support ceased.

In the other case the respondent was in a relationship with a married man who was separated from his wife. Though he offered to get an annulment and marry her, she took the advice of a priest who had counselled her against marriage. She concurred with him that this was not the way she wanted to start a marriage and family life. Her boyfriend's support ceased when she made this decision.

> *"But there were a lot of problems, it would take years for an annulment. And so I finished up the relationship with him and he didn't take it so nicely. I wrote to him, but he never replied." (Res 11)*

What emerges from the above four instances is that these women's choices were circumscribed by a moral agenda which, while promoting the concept of the family, was punitive towards those who did not adhere to the norm of Christian marriage.

(b) Putative father unsupportive. Nine respondents stated that they told the putative father of the pregnancy but no support or realistic support was offered to them. In fact, the response of putative fathers was either to abscond or to renege on the fathering role. One respondent described how when she told her boyfriend, he disappeared:

> *"Well I told him all right and he scarpered fairly quickly."*
> *(Res 6)*

Another respondent told her boyfriend directly, and also had her mother tell his relatives. Neither of these strategies seemed to make him believe he should accept his responsibilities:

> *"The father didn't want to know. I told him and my mother told an aunt of his, and he absconded, he went, he disappeared." (Res 2)*

Two respondents described how they received a reaction but it was completely unsupportive:

> *"When I told him I was pregnant, he as much as told me to run and jump." (Res 7)*

> *"He wanted nothing to do with it." (Res 18)*

One respondent recounted how her boyfriend's lack of support was manifested through his rejecting the help she was offered:

> *"My boyfriend's boss and his wife offered to care for me but his reaction was, 'wouldn't it be better if you stayed with somebody you didn't know?'" (Res 13)*

This respondent's boyfriend offered no other support besides suggesting she did not take help from his colleagues.

One respondent described how the support she was offered was unrealistic when it came to having to manage financially:

> *"I think he gave me something like a fiver (£5) or something ridiculous." (Res 15)*

In recounting their experiences, these respondents were sad and angry about the way they (and their child) had been treated. Their feelings were that they had been "let down" by the putative fathers. The putative fathers' unwillingness to accept responsibility was given as another problem the pregnant women had to deal with as they were trying to make decisions for themselves and their child.

(c) Putative father not told. For the five respondents who did not inform the putative father about the pregnancy, the principal explanations for this non-disclosure were family pressure and a lack of faith in the relationship. Where family pressure was concerned, the young women were denied the opportunity by their parents to tell the putative father. In the instances where the respondents did not have faith in the relationship they made the decision themselves to keep knowledge of the pregnancy from the father.

Respondent 3 recounted how she decided she could not tell the putative father because of the absolute necessity of the pregnancy being kept secret from her parents. She did not trust her boyfriend and said that through him or his parents the information might be passed back to her parents and even throughout the neighbourhood.

One respondent described how she was spirited away to London by her parents before she had a chance to tell her boyfriend.

> *"The guy didn't know I was pregnant, he hadn't got a clue, he didn't know. All he knew was that I vanished off the face of the earth and I was apparently supposed to be over in London." (Res 14)*

Another respondent who was immediately sent to a Mother and Baby Home was denied the opportunity to tell:

> *"I never see the father of the child. I don't know if he knew I was pregnant, I never got a chance to tell him." (Res 8)*

One respondent explained that she did not see the relationship as a long-term one and therefore did not foresee that the father would be involved with her or the child in the long term.

> *"I was 18, he was twice my age. Tricky situation. When I told him I wanted to go out with friends my own age, he took umbrage and so I never heard from him again. He didn't know I was pregnant at the time." (Res 1)*

Whatever the reactions of these putative fathers might have been, they did not have the opportunity to decide whether or not they wanted to be involved in a decision about the pregnancy.

Silencing the Pregnancy

All of the 18 respondents reported that once they had told parents, siblings, friends or boyfriends of their pregnancy the immediate concern was that the pregnancy must be kept secret. Plans of action were immediately formulated and implemented to ensure the pregnancy was hidden. One respondent, reflecting on what it must have been like for her parents, thought that they, like her, must have been feeling afraid:

> *"My parents reaction was fear, where are we going to send her . . . yes, that was their reaction which I suppose, at the time [1976] was absolutely normal." (Res 13)*

Another thought her parents were influenced by the possibility of being socially stigmatised:

> *"And the old-fashioned stigma was there, they were more worried about the neighbours than they were about an individual." (Res 9)*

For one respondent the parental need to conceal the pregnancy from the community overrode other moral taboos and one of her parents actually suggested that she have an abortion.

Elaborate plans and arrangements were thought about, discussed and implemented by parents as ways of ensuring that the pregnancy remained hidden. Assistance to ensure secrecy was sought from priests, social services, relatives and friends and all this was done at great speed.

One respondent, who saw herself as having been forced by her parents to leave home described the haste with which plans were made for her departure:

> *"So literally the following day, I'd say there were three or four phone calls made and the next thing I was being shipped to stay with this man and his wife and their children and I was to stay with them until the baby was born." (Res 14)*

Another respondent who was "housed" elsewhere for the period of her confinement had conditions imposed by her parents as to how she was to communicate with her friends:

> *"I was whisked off to the doctor and whisked off to Dublin and I spent the rest of the time there with a second cousin. I was left up there, I wasn't to ring any of my friends, I wasn't to write to any of my friends, I was cut off from everybody." (Res 7)*

Another respondent who was also sent to stay with a family in Dublin was given a cover story about being in England. She was also given the means to ensure her story rang true:

> *"Things just snowballed. I was leaving home within a couple of weeks, up to Dublin, with a family that were terrible to me. I was in Dublin, but pretending I was in England. I used to send letters to my aunt and she would put an English stamp on them and send them home." (Res 9)*

For five respondents the "solution" to concealing the pregnancy was to live at a Mother and Baby Home until their child was born.

The parents of two respondents insisted they leave home and go to a Mother and Baby Home.

One respondent described how she was sent to the Mother and Baby Home in Roscrea within a few days of her pregnancy being confirmed:

> *"It was a Sunday and I was shipped off and that was that, and I was there for the whole nine months, well over it, I was over a year there, after my son was adopted as well." (Res 8)*

Another respondent was also sent to a home before her pregnancy began to "show". It seemed to this young woman that it was more important for her parents not to be tainted with the social stigma of having an unmarried daughter pregnant at home than for them to care about her welfare.

> *"I was put there because of neighbours, because of what neighbours thought, you know you were evil, you were wrong, you know Litany of Saints was put on to you as well." (Res 2)*

One of the respondents who went to a Mother and Baby Home did so because her mother insisted she did not come home during her pregnancy and a few weeks before she gave birth her doctor suggested it was the best place for her to receive support. Another respondent had not told any of her family and needed the services which the Home offered in order to continue to conceal her pregnancy.

The final respondent had told her sister but again in order to conceal her pregnancy, she had to take refuge within a Home to ensure that no one found out she was pregnant. This respondent gave details of further strategies of concealment which were implemented within these institutions on behalf of the women who were pregnant. Within the Home it was "organised" that her correspondence would go to her mother from where she was supposed to be working:

> *"I would write the post cards and give them to the priest and he had the contact to have them posted in France." (Res 11)*

These comments by the respondents on the strategies and plans they had to make or which were made by parents give an indication of how powerless they found themselves to be upon announcing their crisis pregnancy. Their powerlessness extended to their literally not having any choices about how they were going to deal with this crisis pregnancy.

In disclosing the news of their pregnancies none of these women received affirmation or sufficient support from their families or the putative father to consider keeping their babies. Instead they were confronted with the twin concerns of a) keeping the pregnancy a secret, particularly in the context of the community and b) concealing the pregnancy and birth to the utmost degree possible. In the cases where parents were told, these parents colluded with priests and helping agencies to build a wall of silence around their daughter's "condition". In the other cases boyfriends or the respondents themselves took elaborate measures to ensure secrecy and silence.

The Adoption Decision

All of the mothers recounted how throughout their pregnancy they were scared about the decision that would have to be made once their child was born. No matter what was their age (16 to 31) it was the mothers alone who ultimately had to sign the legal documents relinquishing their child for adoption. None of the mothers, regardless of age or social class, considered they had a real choice when it came to signing the adoption consents.

Sullivan and Groden (1995) describe how for most of the mothers in their study, keeping their babies was not an option. Almost 90 per cent of them said they had no other choice at the time. Parental pressure, finances, lack of support from putative father, marital status, social pressure and age all combined to preclude the option of keeping their babies.

The mothers in this study identified similar reasons for not keeping their babies. The pressures which they mentioned as most influential were: parental and family pressure, pressure from helping agencies and lack of money.

Parental and Family Pressure

The mothers described various ways in which parental and family pressure was experienced. Seven respondents stated categorically that they felt the pressure put on them by their parents was so intense that they did not feel they were responsible for making the adoption decision.

One respondent described her experience when it came to a decision about leaving her baby behind in the Mother and Baby Home:

> "I didn't make that decision. I begged and pleaded with them to bring him home and they said you are not bringing him home, and that is it. They wouldn't look at him, they wouldn't go near him." (Res 2)

Another respondent recounted how, as far as she was concerned, there was no meaningful discussion:

> "I do remember my father saying, 'It is the right decision for you, it is the right decision for us', but there was never an option." (Res 14)

Yet again, as with decisions during their pregnancy, they felt completely powerless:

> "It was my parents' decision, and I just had no choice in what happened, and that was it." (Res 2)

One respondent vividly recounted how she felt when it was time to deal with the final consent to adoption:

> "I won't say I signed, rather I was forced to sign, because as far as I was concerned my son was taken from me, he wasn't given, because I had no choice in the matter, my father saw to all of that." (Res 18)

Projections about the stigma which an illegitimate child would suffer was another form of pressure used by parents with their daughters who might have wanted to keep their child:

> "And my mother kept saying, 'how could you hold on to a child, can you imagine her being called a little bastard, going to school, what would people say, you couldn't do that to a child'." (Res 1)

One respondent absorbed the stigma in relation to herself:

> "An unmarried mother was somebody who, you know, she was kind of easy to get, that was the attitude, and they were kind of looked down on." (Res 11)

Finally, one respondent truly believed that the stigma which attached to her as an unmarried mother could ruin her brother's chances of being ordained to the priesthood:

> "My brother was the biggest influence, he had a wonderful vocation, what would he have done, he would have been kicked out of College on my account." (Res 5)

The sense of powerlessness which these mothers felt was at its most acute when they felt under pressure to sign their child away. The stigma which they felt and which was imposed on them left them feeling vulnerable and helpless.

Pressure from Helping Agencies

According to the accounts given by the respondents, it was not only their families who denied them a real choice in relation to the adoption decision. Professionals and helping agencies with whom they were in contact or from whom they sought advice and assistance, did not offer any options.

One respondent said the safety of her child was threatened:

> "After he was born the social worker had arranged to take him into a home until I was going to decide what to do. But when I

went to see her she actually told me that if I wouldn't take him
out or sign him over for adoption that she would leave him on
the roadside." (Res 10)

Sixteen of the eighteen respondents said they found the agencies
unhelpful. Respondents sought their help in the hope that there
might be some choice, some other solution besides having to part
with their child, but for the majority of them, the perception was
that even the agencies colluded in compelling them towards
adoption:

"In fact looking back, I did have the choice. People who were in
professional areas, they didn't tell the choices that could be
there for a girl." (Res 15)

This respondent had sought assistance and support through a
Mother and Baby Home. She did not recall being given any information on financial assistance or other supports which were
available at the time through the social welfare system.

Financial Pressure

In this study, respondents referred to their concern and worries
about how, from a financial perspective, they could manage to
raise their child alone. They had not been offered any realistic
support from their families or from the putative fathers. None of
the mothers mentioned or seemed to be aware that there was any
state support available, despite the fact that eleven of the mothers
gave birth after the introduction of Unmarried Mothers Allowance in 1973. Even when they asked about financial support, what
was available was not presented to them as a realistic income on
which they could raise their child:

"I remember saying to the social worker, 'I don't know about
this adoption' and she saying to me, 'well do you have any
more money today than you had yesterday?' I said, 'I don't'
and she said, 'well what can you do for a child?' . . . so you see
no matter where I turned . . ." (Res 9)

Some mothers delayed making their decision and requested the agency's help in having their child placed in foster care while they sought solutions. But it seemed that no matter what they tried the odds were stacked against them:

> *"Well I got the adoption agency to get a foster home. I was looking for a way that I could keep working, have enough for a flat, childcare. But there was no way I could make that sort of money." (Res 6)*

> *"I had no job or anything. I hadn't even dole or anything like that. I was borrowing £2 every week from my sister to pay for foster care . . . and there was no work coming up." (Res 16)*

This combination of parental, agency and financial pressures which the respondents experienced during such a vulnerable time resulted in their believing there was no other solution possible beyond relinquishing their child for adoption.

The Impact of Relinquishment

Motherhood Silenced

For a woman who was pregnant and who has just given birth, the "normal" sequence of events is that she brings her child home and begins her life as a mother. The support which was present throughout the pregnancy is likely to continue as the tasks of mothering begin. As described above, the experience of the women in this study was that they did not feel supported throughout their pregnancy. Rather than being an event to celebrate, the pregnancy became a "condition" which had at all costs to be kept secret. Once the children were born, motherhood was swiftly denied as the children were removed within very short periods of time to foster or adoptive care. As the women re-entered the "normal" social world they had inhabited before their pregnancy, it was made clear to them that it was essential to con-

tinue the web of silence around the existence of their child who
had disappeared through adoption.

For the twelve respondents who returned to live with their
parents, definite instructions were immediately issued to ensure
that the discredited action of pregnancy outside marriage remained a secret. Fearful of the stigma that would attach to them
within the neighbourhood if it were known their un-wed daughter had a child, parents took charge and issued commands as to
how the silence was to be maintained:

> *"My father came down and collected me and drove me home.
> He said, 'Straighten yourself up now, think about the
> neighbours. We will never talk about this again'." (Res 14)*

Evidence of how the pregnancy was denied through the elaborate
measures taken to "hide" the pregnant woman were described
above. Once the baby had been relinquished for adoption and
there was no *physical evidence* of its existence, further strategies to
ensure secrecy were imposed on the young women. Denial of the
respondent's experience and the child's existence was secured
through an imposed silence:

> *"It wasn't discussed for 17 years." (Res 1)*

> *"My father said, 'I do not want to hear about you or your bas-
> tard ever again . . . it will not be discussed and you will not be
> asked about it'." (Res 18)*

One respondent recounted how this lack of discussion and denial
about the birth of her child made the whole event seem unreal:

> *"It was never, ever, discussed. Ever. It was like as if it had
> never happened." (Res 12)*

Living with Grief

Once the pregnancy and birth had effectively been silenced, the
respondents were left with their own intense and personal grief as
a result of having parted with their child. In the course of the in-

terviews for this research, when asked to reflect on how living with this grief had affected their lives, the respondents all had a lot to say. One respondent put it graphically when she asked, "How long is your tape?"

Grief is the reaction that follows a significant loss. It is the process that allows for the resolution or partial resolution of the loss. Within the extensive literature on loss and grief Parkes (1991) and Worden (1995) conceptualise grief as having four phases:

1. A period of numbness and denial which occurs close to the time of the loss

2. A period in which a person yearns and searches for the lost one

3. A period when anger and self-reproach for what has happened comes to haunt the bereaved.

4. A period of disorganisation and despair leading eventually to a reorganisation of feelings and reality.

When applying this model of bereavement to the experience of the respondents in this study it is clear that the respondents experienced each of the stages as outlined by Parkes (1991) and Worden (1995). What also emerges however is that there are many ways in which this model falls short of explaining the true impact of the bereavement experience of a mother who relinquished her child.

1. Numbness and denial. Numbness is a common response to shock and is often the mind's way of defending itself against the effects of intense pain and emotional trauma. In many of the biographical accounts of mothers who parted with a child for adoption, numbness and a sense of total detachment from others and the world around them were common reactions to the emotional turmoil in which they found themselves after they had relinquished their child (Musser, 1979; Batts, 1994; Wells, 1994; Wadia-Ells, 1996; Powell and Warren, 1997; Robson, 2000).

All of the respondents in this study recounted how, because of their need to "close down" at the time, they now had difficulties recalling many of the details around the birth of their child. They found they often could not recall specific details such as how long they were in labour, the time of birth or the weight of their child. One respondent said she had a complete void:

> *"The actual birth is blank, I have a complete blank about going into the delivery." (Res 1)*

For five respondents' memories of the circumstances of handing over their child were hazy:

> *"And we brought her to the agency . . . and into a room, and that was it. And after that I don't remember one thing." (Res 13)*

In times of intense trauma, denial, which involves the suppression of reality, is a mechanism which the mind and body use to survive what is happening. When mothers were faced with the pain of parting with a child to whom they had just given birth, they often closed down and denied what was happening. Powell and Warren (1997) suggest that as a result of the pain experienced at the time of relinquishment it is common for natural mothers to be unable to remember even very significant details surrounding the adoption. For nine respondents in this study one example of such suppression was that there was limited or no recall of the crucial act of signing the documents to finally and legally relinquish their motherhood:

> *"I remember going into court and signing a book, well I thought it was a book, I don't know what it was, that is all I remember. I don't remember how I got there or I don't remember who I saw there." (Res 5)*

> *"I don't remember signing the papers at all." (Res 15)*

The interviews for this study took place between 20 and 40 years after relinquishment. Despite wanting to be able to piece their lives together again, and to have the full "story" of birth and relinquishment for their child, mothers were still unable to recall details of what had been a very traumatic and painful period. The numbness, isolation and sense of unreality about all that had happened had not shifted significantly. The pain and sadness experienced as a result of adoption appeared to intensify rather than diminish.

2. Yearning and searching. Yearning for the one who has died to return is described by Parkes (1991) as a normal stage in the bereavement process. For the majority (17)[1] of the respondents in this study the yearning for their absent child manifested itself in longing to know, or wondering what had happened to their child:

> *"I kept thinking every day about where was he gone, who had him, was he in Ireland or where was he . . . they never told you anything." (Res 8)*

> *"You always were, you know, when you saw other children growing up, you would be looking into a pram, or when you saw children on the beach, you would wonder what your child was doing." (Res 16)*

As a rule, the bereaved can acknowledge that the search for the dead person is irrational and futile although the impulse to do so is strong. For mothers who have parted with their children for adoption this urge to search is complicated. Their searching impulses are not irrational, their child is still alive and the possibility of a future meeting or contact is more than a fantasy.

For many mothers in the years post-adoption the ongoing pain and sadness of relinquishment intensifies rather than diminishes

---

[1] One respondent, because her child had been adopted by the foster carers, knew where her child lived. For a number of years after the adoption she also received information from the adoptive parents about how her child was progressing.

(Howe et al., 1992; Wells, 1990; Watson, 1986). For the respondents in this study the experience was similar:

> *"It was 20 years for me, I mean every single year. I was in bits every September, all through the 20 years, every September was terrible, every Christmas was terrible."* (Res 12)

Unlike the fantasies and dreams of a person who is mourning death and who for whom there is rationale to accepting the irreversible nature of death, for the relinquishing mother there was no finality, no closure or no possibility of closure. Their child continued to exist and as a result the mothers' yearning made sense and was rational.

3. Anger and self-reproach. Parkes (1991) and Worden (1995) describe how for the bereaved, anger and self-reproach are most often part of the constellation of feelings during the period when they are coming to terms with their loss. They are often angry with themselves for not having done enough to prevent the loss. Winkler and Van Keppel (1982) found that feelings of anger, self-reproach, shame and guilt are to the forefront of the experience of mothers who have relinquished a child. The mother feels responsible for the decision to give up her child and therefore feels the loss as a self-inflicted one. Robson (2000) suggests that this ongoing anger and self-reproach results in ongoing feelings of guilt, shame and powerlessness.

Respondents in this study described their own pain and how they reproached themselves:

> *"I am very sorry for parting with her, very, very, sorry. I am sure there was some way out if I had really tried hard enough."* (Res 11)

One respondent felt she deserved to be castigated:

> *"I always felt secretly when I was expecting my second child that I wouldn't have another girl. I always felt that God would punish me for giving her away."* (Res 7)

For another respondent the consequences of relinquishment took on a religious significance:

> *"I always felt I had done a terrible thing, that it was a major*
> *sin, a major sin. The darkness was always there." (Res 14)*

Respondents described how they were often embarrassed because they used to think people were talking about what they had done. They described feelings of paranoia, they did not want to go out and mix with friends, they felt ashamed and embarrassed about having given up their child.

A key component of shaming is a message to the other that they are dishonourable and unworthy of respect. Shaming may be institutionalised in social stigma but it is most wounding when it occurs at the hands of somebody we want to please. Nowhere is this more apparent than in the relationship between parent and child (Loader, 1997). When trying to reconcile their own feelings of loss with their feelings of self-reproach for parting with their child, mothers often worried about how their child would feel about their illegitimate and adoptive status:

> *"Not only did I bring this terrible shame to me, but I brought*
> *this terrible burden to him as well." (Res 14)*

A woman whose mothering aims and expectations have been frustrated or denied often experiences a sense of exclusion, shame and loneliness (Leon, 1998). For the respondents in this study, these feelings did not abate with time and led to complications in their grieving and unresolved issues in the bereavement process.

4. Disorganisation and reorganisation. For the bereaved adjusting to life without the person who has died involves a period of turmoil and confusion, and eventually a re-adjustment and reorganisation. The absent person is re-incorporated into their lives as someone who lived and has now died. There is a recognition of what has happened and of the new reality (Parkes, 1991; Worden, 1995). However, for mothers who parted with their children the advice they received was to go on with their lives or to put the child out of their minds and to forget about what had happened (Watson, 1986; Howe et al., 1992; Wells, 1990). All of the respondents in this study described how in the immediate period after relinquishment they felt confused and overwhelmed by the enormous loss they had just experienced. They described how their reality was that they had just become mothers, but their child, although real and alive, was no longer with them. As they tried to reorganise and get on with their lives, the bereavement process became complicated for them as a result of the denial of their experience and fact that their child was absent. They were constantly engaged in the management of the impression that there was no child and that adoption did not have an impact on their lives. One respondent described how at different junctures in her life reorganisation was extremely difficult because of the denial involved:

> "You had a mask on the whole time, you were the happiest person in this world, and your heart was breaking, but what could you do?" (Res 5)

In very practical ways she described how the denial had to be managed:

> "I didn't do anything with my girlfriends. I wouldn't dare even change my nurse's uniform because of the stretch marks. I was hiding myself the whole time." (Res 5)

And this continued at a most important juncture of her life:

> "When I got married and had my baby I went to a hospital in Dublin because I thought it was best to have my second baby in Dublin, rather than pretending that it was my first in the town where I lived because all my friends were nursing." (Res 5)

One respondent stated that over the course of her life the imposition of silence about her child had been so intense and absolute that she no longer felt she had the words needed to express her thoughts and feelings about him or what had happened to him.

Another respondent described how, throughout her life, articulating the answer to questions about the number of children she had was difficult:

> *"And mentally you are thinking, I have another girl. You are saying you have two children, but you have three, but really you only have two." (Res 13)*

The mothers in this study who lost children through adoption were never given permission to grieve. The silencing of their motherhood led to the suppression of emotions and a denial of their experience. Their loss had never been validated and so a true resolution of their grief could not begin. The consequences of this distorted grief was to have profound and long-lasting effects.

Efforts Made to Regain Control

When describing how they survived in the years post-relinquishment, ten of the mothers gave details of how they made efforts to try to relieve part of their pain. They hoped they might regain some measure of control if they tried to do something practical to ensure they were contactable if their child ever requested information about them. The respondents thought that if they kept the adoption agency informed of any change of address, a change of name through marriage, or other changes in their circumstances, then if their child was ever to enquire about them, the agency would have the correct and up-to-date information as to how they could be contacted.

When mothers did write to agencies with their up-to-date personal information and details, however, they were often thwarted in their efforts:

> *"So I wrote the agency ten years ago, and I heard nothing. So I wrote again, just to make sure that the letter had not gone astray, and they finally wrote back to say it had not." (Res 13)*

One respondent found that she had to become particularly assertive with the agency in order to ensure her up-to-date details were

recorded. She eventually had to send a solicitor's letter which elicited an immediate reply.

Other respondents described how they sent letters, photographs, birthday and Christmas cards to their children through
the agency. They seemed to be aware that the agencies would not
pass on this correspondence (they stated that they hoped it would
be retained on file), but they wanted their child to know they had
tried to communicate with them throughout the years. With the
exception of one respondent who was given a small amount of
information by a social worker, none of the other respondents
who made efforts to keep in touch could say they received any
acknowledgements of their correspondence to the agencies concerned. The powerlessness of their position was thus further reinforced through the silence of the agencies.

Eight respondents recounted how they did not even attempt to
make any contact in the years post-relinquishment. For some
mothers, the protective strategies and rationalisations they employed to deny the pain of parting with their child remained
throughout the following years. Their sense of powerlessness did
not diminish:

> *"Throughout the pregnancy I always thought this child is for
> someone else, I know that is terrible, but that is the way it
> was." (Res 3)*

> *"She belonged to someone else, I had no rights." (Res 5)*

For these women to try to think of themselves as the mother of
their absent child was just too painful. They could never allow
themselves explore the possibility of trying to re-establish contact
and so never became proactive in attempting to contact the
agency.

Two respondents said they did not know or remember the
name of the adoption agency which had handled the adoption of
their child. They believed that it was absolutely forbidden for
them ever to try to make contact; they said they had been told this
at the time of relinquishment. They longed to know about their

child, but believed they had no legal or moral right to have any information. For these respondents the pain of parting with their child had remained so overwhelming throughout their lives that they were never able to contemplate that they might be instrumental in initiating a reunion. Their sense of powerlessness was acute, extreme and long-lasting.

Summary

To be single and pregnant was perceived and experienced as a crisis for all of the respondents in this study. Support and assistance which might have resulted in their becoming single mothers was not available. Instead, pressure to relinquish their child for adoption was the solution offered to the existence of an illegitimate child. There was no real choice offered to mothers despite their age or social class. Adoption proved to be a painful experience and overall the respondents described long lasting and negative effects on their lives and personalities as a result of parting with a child. Their particular form of motherhood was painfully silenced. These accounts are of the experience of mothers in Ireland during the 1950s, 1960s and 1970s. They are very real stories of very real tragedies. These accounts give an important insight into the emotional consequences of giving up a child at birth and how, for the mother who relinquishes her child through adoption, the situation is irretrievable.

Chapter 5

MOTHER AND CHILD REUNITED

"You are feeling so wonderful that this person is there, your first born, your daughter is there. You thought it would never happen, and you are looking, she is talking, you just cannot believe it." (Res 5)

A key event in the life of any woman who relinquished a child for adoption is the prospect or anticipation of a possible reunion with her child. The event of a reunion is more than a meeting between mother and child who have been separated for many years. Rather, it is a complex process which begins with initial contact between both parties and continues right through to the possible establishment of a relationship after meeting. Heightened emotions and expectations make it a highly charged event which can be both liberating and exhausting (McColm, 1993).

This chapter describes the direct experience of the actual reunion process for the respondents. The emotions and reactions which the mothers had when they were initially contacted by the adoption agency are explored and described. Their preparation for and anticipation of the reunion is related in their own words. The respondents give their own personal account of the actual reunion meeting, an event which was emotionally charged and a traumatic event for both mother and child. Finally, the respondents give details of how they experienced the services of the agency which facilitated their reunion.

Closed Adoption

The children of the respondents in this study were all adopted under a system of closed adoption. In closed adoption, the mother who gave birth had no legal right to any information or contact with her child after she signed the final consent to adoption. As was explained in the Introduction, she had relinquished all her rights to and responsibilities for her child through the adoption contract.

Despite efforts made by the respondents to keep agencies informed of their circumstances, for 16 of the 18 respondents there had been absolutely no news or information about their child over periods ranging from 20 to 40 years.[1] The median number of years spent by the respondents not knowing anything about their absent child was 21 years. All of the respondents described these long periods of time as having been filled with a constant longing to have some news or information. They wondered where their child was, how they had fared in their adoptive family, and whether they were happy. They often wondered whether their child was alive or dead.

For the 18 mothers in this study, the prospect of and opportunity for a reunion with their child eventually became an option. Five mothers who persisted in their attempts to be the one to initiate contact were eventually facilitated in this process by the agency. One mother, who happened to approach the agency when her child was 25, was facilitated with her wish to make contact. For the other 12 mothers, contact was made with them when their child requested that the agency facilitate a reunion.

---

[1] Two respondents had received some information. One child was in foster care for two years before her mother decided to sign the consent to the adoption. During this period the mother had contact with their child and the foster parents. When the final consent was signed the adoptive mother continued to send news and information to the natural mother on an annual basis until the child requested a meeting at age 16. In the other instance, the natural mother was in contact with the adoption agency in order to place a birthday card on her son's file. She spoke with a social worker who informed her that she had visited the adoptive home and that her child was well and happy.

Table 5.1: Who Initiated Contact

Who Initiated Contact	Numbers
Contact initiated by mothers	6
Contact initiated by adoptees	12
Total	18

An adoption reunion is often focused upon as a single event. As will emerge through the accounts of these respondents, however, it is actually a process of several stages, each of which has emotional consequences for the mother and her child.

The respondents identified four stages which had particular impact and significance for them:

- Contact initiated through the agency

- Anticipation and preparation for reunion meeting

- The reunion meeting

- Post-reunion.

The respondents' accounts on the first three stages will be outlined in this section. Their accounts of the post-reunion experience will be given in the following section.

Contact Initiated through the Adoption Agency

The event of being contacted by an agency on behalf of their child, or finally being successful in having the agency begin the search on their own behalf, brought about dramatic changes in the emotions and attitudes of the respondents.

For one respondent it was as if her son who had been dead became real again:

> *"It really brought it home to me when I got the photos that he really does exist." (Res 3)*

In comparison to the ongoing suppression of their emotions to which they had felt obliged to subscribe since relinquishment, they now described how their emotions became alive and real again:

> *"I was on Cloud 9, on tenterhooks, and the excitement was unbelievable." (Res 9)*

> *"It was very exciting, very exciting, very little sleep because when I went to bed at night I always thought about him and it was very emotional."(Res 10)*

For one respondent her emotional state reached manic proportions:

> *"It was just pure elation, I just couldn't sleep. I was just on a high, my head was going mad. I was full of emotional energy, and it lasted for months." (Res 5)*

And for some it was emotionally a very trying time:

> *"I just broke down, I just broke down." (Res 2)*

One respondent went on to explain how she had to "read, read, read" about the experiences of other mothers in order to reassure herself that she was not losing her mind and to begin to feel grounded again.

All of the respondents said that during this period after initial contact their moods fluctuated. Sometimes they were "as high as kites" and sometimes depressed and upset. They had difficulties sleeping. When recounting their emotional state, they remembered that they had difficulty concentrating and so found it hard to work. They became self-absorbed and said how they often resented having to find time for the rest of their family. They became obsessed with the prospect of the reunion meeting. The respondents all described it as a period of intense emotional turmoil.

Anticipating and Preparing for the Reunion

Most importantly for these mothers, the fact that there was contact with an agency meant that their child was now expressing a
wish to meet them and there was a *real* possibility of a reunion.
According to Robinson (2000), the prospect of an adoption reunion is a key emotional experience, which will most likely be filled
with a range of positive and negative emotions. For the respondents in this study, happiness and joy in anticipation of a reunion
were some of the key sentiments expressed.

> *"Oh, it was a brilliant time, it was a time I would love to have
> again, the anticipation was just so great, it really was, like a
> child waiting for Christmas." (Res 13)*

> *"It was very exciting, to me it was very exciting. I was totally
> and utterly on a high. I was bursting with excitement." (Res 7)*

Robinson (2000) also draws attention to how the prospect of reunion brings back "the feelings of emptiness, loss and sadness the
mothers felt when they were first separated from their children".
The respondents in this study described similar emotions:

> *"I did feel a lot of pain, it is hard to describe really. He was
> nearly a year old when he was adopted and I hadn't seen him
> since and it all came back to me." (Res 8)*

> *"A lot of pain, a lot of anger, a lot of hurt came through . . .
> you know after 21 years you had found him. The anger, the
> hurt, everything just kept flowing through." (Res 2)*

As described earlier these mothers had had to manage and suppress their emotions throughout the years post-relinquishment.
Ongoing feelings of grief, pain and anger had become normalised
for them. They now began to realise they had buried their sadness
and anger. For some it was a surprise to find their anger resurfaced intensely:

> *"I got very emotional, I got very upset with my parents, for what happened. I was full of aggression for Mammy." (Res 7)*

The respondents also identified how they experienced fears in anticipation of meeting their child. The desire of these respondents that their child "approve" of them at the meeting was acute. They worried about the impression they would create:

> *"Oh my God, I was up to ninety, I was up to ninety, and I was saying, 'what will I wear, what will I say'?" (Res 15)*

The fears they had were compounded with feelings of guilt and shame which re-surfaced for them when they were confronted with the real possibility of a reunion:

> *"How could I possibly start now to meet someone I had given away. I could not ask him to forgive me, I just didn't know where to start." (Res 17)*

Anticipating and preparing for the reunion meeting was a difficult and extremely stressful time for the respondents. Their emotions were raw and unpredictable. They were excited at the prospect of a meeting but the sadness, grief and guilt which they felt about parting with their child resurfaced acutely for them.

The Reunion Meeting

When describing their reunion meetings, respondents gave details of how each individual reunion meeting had been set up differently. Twelve reunions took place in the office an agency, six took place in a café or a hotel. The length of time for which the respondents and their children met also varied, ranging from an hour and a half to a full day.

Despite their fears and apprehensions, 16 of the 18 respondents described how, though full of emotional turmoil, from their point of view, the meeting went well:

> *"It was a joyful occasion, again mixed emotions." (Res 11)*

"We just got on really well, it was absolutely great." (Res 13)

One respondent described how the time spent together flew:

"We were there for I suppose for three hours and then we went off to lunch and it was just like five minutes." (Res 9)

And another described needing much more time than she anticipated to tell her story:

"We met and then we spent the evening, and we had a meal, and we were just talking and talking and the next day we arranged to meet and it was the same thing, we talked again." (Res 10)

Their worries about whether they should avoid physical contact were overtaken by instinctive reactions:

"We just flew into each others arms." (Res 5)

"I walked in and I just grabbed him and hugged him." (Res 9)

"He just came straight to me and I went straight to him." (Res 12)

In conjunction with these feelings of elation, respondents also described how, as the meeting progressed it was hard to accept that they were actually and finally face to face with their grown-up child. What was happening was real, but in some strange way, it was also unreal. Respondents described how they experienced a sense of detachment:

"The feelings of your inner self, you're kind of cool on the outside, but your inner self, you keep on saying, 'its not true, is it real?'" (Res 5)

One respondent described how the feelings of loneliness and isolation which had been attached to the secrecy and silencing of her pregnancy came back to haunt her during the meeting. This respondent had never told anyone in her family of origin that she had placed a child for adoption, nor had she told her husband or the children of her marriage. The continued secrecy about the existence of her child made the reunion meeting very difficult both practically and emotionally:

> "It was all done in secret, the morning of my reunion my husband had gone out of the country for the day at 9.30 am and I had the reunion at 11.30 am. It was hectic. It was very emotional, very, very emotional. I'll never forget it. When I saw him walking into the room my whole life flashed in front of me, because the last time I had seen him was when I had parted with him in hospital." (Res 3)

And another respondent described how she was unable to control her emotions:

> "It was just that I cried my eyes out, it's just I don't know what came over me. I am sure there were a lot of people in the hotel wondering what we were at . . . there was great sadness involved." (Res 16)

Despite their hopes and wishes for a successful reunion two respondents did not believe their meeting went well. One of these respondents described how, despite her intentions, she became immobilised both physically and emotionally at the meeting:

> "Like I had it all planned in my head how it was going to be. And when I arrived in she was there and I think I froze. I had been very keep not to overpower her . . . but with hindsight I am very sorry that I didn't give her a hug. She was awkward and I was awkward." (Res 1)

Another respondent described how she found it difficult to get beyond her terror, which overrode any other feelings she had:

> "I have never been more terrified in my life. I saw her sitting there and I just wanted to turn around and walk out. I don't really know what I felt, there wasn't really anything." (Res 6)

The emotional experience of the meeting was overpowering for these two respondents. As discussed earlier, Parkes (1991) and Worden (1995) identify this feeling of "numbness" as an element of the bereavement process. For these respondents, the feelings which had been so painful when they initially parted with their child were reactivated in an intense and powerful way.

All of the respondents provided vivid accounts of the emotional turmoil they experienced as the meeting with their child drew to a close. They were worn out by the depth of emotion and energy it had been necessary to call upon to get this far.

The guilt they felt about relinquishing their child resurfaced. These feelings were compounded by new feelings of guilt and sadness about what was now actually happening:

> *"When he was leaving and saying goodbye, I looked at him and I thought, well it is your turn to leave me now, to leave me standing here, like what I did to you all those years previously." (Res 3)*

Emotionally they felt relieved that they had survived the meeting:

> *"I suppose some relief that she didn't ask any questions, I was frightened that she would turn around and say, 'you are a right cow, what the hell did you give me up for?'" (Res 6)*

And their fears for the future were already forming:

> *"I just had that awful feeling that maybe that's it, she has met me now and that's it." (Res 13)*

> *"Oh it was absolutely horrendous leaving because you didn't know would you ever see him again." (Res 9)*

Agency Service in Connection with Reunion

As outlined in Chapter 3, the respondents for this study were recruited through five agencies which facilitate adoption reunions. During the process of reunion, however, some of the respondents used more than one agency. They availed of the services of a second agency either because they were dissatisfied with the service offered by the agency which had handled their adoption or because they lived a great distance from that agency. As a result the comments in this section relate to the respondents' experience of seven agencies. The two extra agencies about which comments were made were registered adoption societies. The respondents were asked directly to comment on the service they got from the agencies and to elaborate on areas of the service which were satisfactory or unsatisfactory. They were asked for their comments in relation to the service received at initial contact with their child; the preparation for the reunion meeting and the service at the reunion meeting.

For all the agencies about which comments were made, there were areas of the service which the respondents found helpful and unhelpful. In addition, there were areas where the respondents believed that the agency treated them with respect and others where they found the agencies' approach or policies to be controlling and disempowering.

Agency Service at Initial Contact

When describing their feelings about being in contact with an adoption agency again after so many years the respondents used words like "daunting", "scary" and "intimidating". Most of the respondents were approaching the agency with a history of previous contact, a contact, they had not, in the majority of instances, found to be helpful. For all of the respondents, dealing with the agency brought back vivid memories of the crisis pregnancy and the adoption process:

> "I found it hard really, it brought back memories." (Res 3)

> "When I was inside the door it was like the day I was there when I had to sign papers." (Res 18)

Ten respondents who were contacted by the agency on behalf of their child commented on how the approach was made. For two respondents this was respectful and empowering:

> *"The way she went about contacting me, it was the right way, she came straight to me. I think that was the proper way, she dealt directly with me. The phone call, she was very discreet, because she rang the day before, and my husband answered the phone and she didn't leave a name and just said she would ring back again." (Res 12)*

> *"She treated me like an adult and I was able to make up my own mind." (Res 13)*

For three respondents the opposite was the case. The agency did not appear to realise how shocking and traumatic it was for a mother to be contacted out of the blue after so many years:

> *"And when she contacted me originally she just rang and left a message, 'Would you please ask your wife to contact me Wednesday morning', . . . so she expected me to wait Friday, Saturday, Sunday, Monday, Tuesday, Wednesday, six days before I could phone." (Res 18)*

In another case the approach lacked sensitivity about the respondent's entitlement to privacy and confidentiality. The social worker from the agency called to the mother's home and since she was not home left a message with her family that she would phone the following day. The respondent was puzzled as to what was going on and even the phone call the next day did not help:

> *"And so she rang the next day, real early, and she told me she wanted to speak to me, private, and it puzzled me, you know, who was she and where was she from?" (Res 8)*

This respondent felt that the way she was approached broke all the rules and boundaries of confidentiality. This was a very real issue for this respondent because although she lived with her mother since the adoption, her mother had never been sympathetic or helpful in relation to her pregnancy. Indeed her child had never been mentioned over a period of 22 years. She was upset therefore that her private business was exposed to her family before she had been consulted.

And finally one respondent felt that, at the initial interview prior to reunion, there was a lack of concern as to how she as a natural mother had managed over the intervening years:

> *"There was no such thing as how did you get on over the years, none of that kind of thing." (Res 9)*

Agency Service during Preparation for Reunion

The majority (16) of respondents were encouraged by the agencies to enter into written correspondence and to exchange photographs in preparation for the actual meeting. As the agencies explained to the respondents, the purpose of writing letters and exchanging photographs was to give the mothers and their children an opportunity to introduce themselves to each other over a period of time. This was seen as being preferable to immediately being immersed in a very highly charged reunion meeting with a person who was related but a stranger. The respondents who did write and exchange photographs found this to be exciting, helpful and valuable:

> *"When I read her letter it was kind of imprinted on your heart forever more. It was a wonderful feeling." (Res 5)*

> *"And her letters were, I don't know, they just hit the right spot." (Res 13)*

It was the policy of some agencies to read the letters before passing them on. Respondents said they found this policy and practice of the agency to be controlling and an infringement on their personal privacy. One respondent expressed how angry it made her to be treated in this manner:

> *"My letters, they did read them. It was like being a child. I felt that way, not as an adult, it wasn't good enough. I felt they were controlling my life. . . . I was the one who should be in*

charge, not them. I was second fiddle. I was very resentful . . ."
(Res 11)

Another respondent stated that she knew she was disempowered by the practice but said that at the time she would have done anything asked of her to ensure contact with her daughter continued. She said that having her letters read made her feel like she had to pass a test to prove she was all right to meet her child.

Despite being dissatisfied with a number of areas of the practice of some agencies, all the respondents in this study stated that for them, it was important to have someone with knowledge and information about the area of adoption reunion available to support them throughout the process. As one respondent described it:

> *"The support from a stranger, your children are marvellous at that time, but the support from a stranger puts the icing on it . . . you are writing and getting to know each other, and then having chats with the social worker, you know you are doing it right and that you are not doing it wrong." (Res 5)*

For the respondents it was important that the agency offer support and assistance to their child and some expressed their satisfaction about the way this was done:

> *"The social worker was incredible. I felt that she was on his side and she was on my side. She was doing this for us." (Res 14)*

> *"Looking back I think she was wonderful, she was very worried about me and concerned about me, and she was concerned about both sides." (Res 11)*

Two respondents expressed praise for the agencies in the way they prepared them for the various possible outcomes:

> *"She told me this is the way it could happen, he may not get on with you, and I think it is a good and relevant point." (Res 2)*

"When I met her she pointed out that it could go very well or very badly and you want to be prepared, and are you sure you want to do this?" (Res 14)

Agency Service at Reunion Meeting

For the respondents it was important that a social worker from the agency was available on the day of reunion. It was appreciated when support was offered:

"When I was going into the reunion I was very nervous and the social worker was there, and I was grand then." (Res 8)

But it was also important that the assistance offered did not interfere with the privacy which the respondents felt the meeting deserved:

"At the reunion I felt she should have left the room, because I remember thinking, as I was hugging him, she was standing watching me." (Res 18)

"And when my son arrived she went out and brought him in, and I think the social worker is a very sentimental person because she literally backed back to the door, and stood there for 30 seconds, and I can remember thinking to myself at the time, 'She is not going to miss this'." (Res 14)

And one respondent, looking back, thought it would have been more sensitive of the agency to suggest a different venue than their office for the meeting:

"And with regard to the reunion, I think I would have preferred to have been elsewhere rather than that place, because it was kind of, it was the room where I had had bad feelings, so I would have preferred it to be somewhere neutral, somewhere totally different." (Res 15)

At the time when these interviews were being carried out, only one of the agencies offered a support group for natural mothers who were in the process of reunion. Four of the respondents were attending this group, all four of whom were respondents who had been dissatisfied with the service offered by the agency which had initially handled the adoption. The support received through speaking to other mothers who were preparing for reunion or who had been through a reunion was described by all of the mothers as extremely useful. The respondents were able to relate to the other group members' feelings of excitement and anticipation about a forthcoming reunion. They were also able to understand the depth of loss and sorrow at having parted with a child for adoption.

Summary

For all of the respondents the experience of being reconnected with their child and having a reunion meeting was an extremely intense and emotional time. The respondents, who might have been expected to feel only happiness and elation about meeting their child, were conscious that it was not that simple. They, who had parted with their children so many years previously, were full of fear and apprehension that their child would be angry because they had abandoned them. They were also fearful that their child would not like them and as a result no relationship could or would develop. Guilt and sadness about the decision which had been made again became intense. The complexity and consequences of the reunion was something they understood and appreciated. The service offered by the agencies was in most instances helpful, but there were aspects to the manner in which it was offered which were disempowering and controlling.

Chapter 6

LIFE AFTER REUNION

"I suppose for the fact that you were not ever able to talk about it for all those years, not able to express your feelings, or the heartache that you carried, that grief that you had and no one knew, and you were not able to talk about your own child to family and neighbours." (Res 16)

Studies undertaken in England, the United States and Australia suggest that the hard work of reunion begins after the initial meeting (Cotton and Parish, 1987; Gediman and Browne, 1991; Field, 1990). The initial reunion meeting must be considered as just the start of a process of readjustment and perhaps integration of a child into the life of the natural mother. There are no established rules or models for post-reunion relationships. According to McColm (1993) once the reunion had taken place natural mothers and their children must create their own definitions of who they are in relation to one another and how they will integrate themselves into each other's lives. The process of establishing and maintaining relationships between mothers and their children who have been absent for many years is complex. Finding the balance which is satisfactory to both sides is difficult and involves compromise and negotiation.

This chapter gives details of the mothers' emotions and how they coped immediately after the reunion meeting. Details of how the relationships between mothers and children have developed are explored. Factors which appeared to influence the development of relationships are examined. The respondents' reflections on how adoption and reunion has affected their lives are recounted.

Emotions Immediately after Reunion

The complexities of the reunion process were evident in the respondents' descriptions of their own emotional states and reactions immediately after their first meeting. Their own expectations and those of families and friends might have been that they would be completely satisfied, content and happy that they had found and met with their child. All the respondents however described how this was a very difficult period for them because of the sense of ambiguity which they experienced and which they had not anticipated. The happiness and euphoria they felt was constrained by very real worries as to whether or how the relationship with their child would develop. They knew they did not have control over this and they had no way of knowing if the relationship they desired would be reciprocated. Consequently, they were often in a state of high anxiety.

One respondent described how she was "taken over" by the process, her whole life became controlled as she waited for her son to initiate the next meeting:

> "I wouldn't leave the phone, we were to go out for a meal that week, I wouldn't go out in case the phone would ring, it was absolutely desperate." (Res 9)

Another respondent worried about whether she had lived up to her daughter's expectations:

> "And then for a while afterwards, while I was waiting to hear from her again, I went on a downer, I went down, you know, 'was she happy with me, did she like me, did she want to meet me again?'" (Res 7)

Yet another respondent described becoming obsessed:

> *"The first six months when I met him I hadn't a clue. I cannot remember a thing about it, all I know is that I was on a high. I was going to work, I know I was mouthing, I never shut up about him, I just kept talking and talking and talking about him all the time." (Res 18)*

The reunion had presented the respondents with an opportunity to revisit their past and their identity as a young mother. One respondent described how it led to conflict with the identity and role she now had:

> *"I sort of reverted back to what I was 20 years ago. I felt I had my identity back as a single person. I went back to that stage, and I was doing what I wanted to do and I didn't care about anyone else. I didn't even want to be married." (Res 12)*

For all the respondents the task of embodying their identity as the mother of an adopted child who had been absent for so many years with their present identity was complex and difficult. A tremendous amount of emotional energy was required to achieve this task. During this turbulent period post-reunion all of the respondents experienced a range of emotions from euphoria to despair. For all of them it was a difficult and stressful time.

Developing a Relationship

The findings of previous research studies on reunions have all pointed to a majority of mothers being pleased that when offered the opportunity, they had gone through with a reunion meeting. This was the case even in situations where the reunion and the development of a relationship had not worked out to their hopes and expectations (Cotton and Parish, 1987; Slaytor, 1988; Silverman, 1988; Field, 1990; Gediman and Browne, 1991; Sullivan, 1995; Mullender and Kearn, 1997; McMillan and Irving, 1997). In most situations contact immediately post-reunion was usually quite frequent but became less frequent or ceased as time progressed (Cotton and Parish, 1986; Mullender and Kearn, 1997; McMillan and Irving, 1997; Feast and Howe, 2000).

In this study, at the time of interview 16 of the 18 respondents continued to have a relationship and ongoing contact with their child. For ten of the respondents, their own perception was that the relationship with their child was a good one and was progressing well. For six respondents, though still in contact with their child, their perception was that there were ongoing difficulties in the relationship. For two respondents the relationship with their child had ceased.

In the ten cases where the relationship was satisfactory, four of the reunions had been initiated by the mother and six by the child. In the six cases where the relationship was not satisfactory two relationships had been the mother and four by the child. In the two instances where the relationship had ceased the contact had been initiated by the child (see Table 6.1).

Table 6.1: Status of Relationship and Who Initiated Contact

Who Initiated Contact	Relationship Satisfactory	Relationship Unsatisfactory	Relationship Ceased
Mother	4	2	—
Child	6	4	2

In this study, a higher proportion of reunions seemed to be satisfactory when initiated by the child (six out of ten). On the other hand, in relationships that were perceived by mothers to be not working well, four had been initiated by the child and two by the mothers. The two relationships which had ceased and by implication were not working had also been initiated by the child.

In the ten relationships that were working well, four respondents were one year post-reunion, four respondents were two years post-reunion, one respondent was five years post-reunion and one respondent was nine years post-reunion. In the six relationships that were not working well, two respondents were one year post-reunion, two respondents were two years post-reunion and in the other two cases the respondents were four and five years post-reunion respectively. In the two cases where the relationships had ceased, one respondent was one year post-reunion and the other was six years post-reunion (see Table 6.2). In relation to the length of time since reunion, no particular pattern of satisfaction or dissatisfaction with the relationship could be discerned across the respondents.

Table 6.2: Status of Relationship and Length of Time since Reunion

Years since Reunion	Relationship Satisfactory	Relationship Unsatisfactory	Relationship Ceased
1	4	2	1
2	4	2	–
4	–	1	–
5	1	1	–
6	–	–	1
9	1	–	–

Relationship Satisfactory

At the time of interview, ten mothers evaluated their relationships with their child as working well. In analysing the data it became clear that a number of key factors determined the likelihood of a satisfactory relationship developing between mother and child. The most important of these were:

- Patterned and predictable structure within the relationship

- Relationship built on friendship

- Acceptance of child's adoptive status

- Interaction and relationships with other children born to the respondent.

Patterned and Predictable

When the relationship between respondent and the adoptee was surrounded by a predictable and patterned structure which the respondent could believe in and rely on, the relationship was going well. Ten respondents reported such a structure to the relationship and as a result their confidence and trust in the relationship was high. One respondent, who was nine years post-reunion, described how it was organised that she sees her son three or four times a year.

> *"Oh it has worked out, definitely it has worked out, for both parties. We meet up, he visits, I visit. He meets me and he leaves me back again, whatever the arrangements would be, we're in touch to arrange by phone." (Res 10)*

This respondent also described the relationship with her son as one of friendship. She knows that he is happy and doing well and the relationship is one of mutual respect for the other's privacy and independence. She knows about him and his life and also knows that she has been accepted as part of it. She trusts that contact will continue. She says that she has been able to put the past behind her and be positive and confident about the relationship.

One respondent, whose child lived outside Ireland, described the pattern which had developed in her relationship:

> *"We have been writing every fortnight or oftener, depending on what is happening . . . and then we met in Wales, and she is coming over here in the summer." (Res 5)*

Two other respondents recounted how they have been able to build on their relationships through regular telephone conversations. One respondent was initially tentative and nervous about contact but things developed and she said as time goes on she has become more confident and she can begin to believe the relationship will last.

The other respondent was sufficiently confident to be relaxed about taking the initiative or waiting for her child to do so:

> *"I cannot go any more than two weeks without giving her a buzz and I know that she can't either. If I don't ring her she will ring me, so I kind of know she needs to talk to me every now and then and I need to talk to her . . . I know the contact is there and I am not afraid of it." (Res 7)*

Relationship Built on Friendship

High levels of satisfaction were reported by nine respondents who said their relationship with their child closely resembled a friendship. These respondents stated they had worked on creating a relationship that was based on friendship rather than one figured around the roles of mother and child:

> *"We are the best of friends, we have better than mother and son relationship in the sense that I can tell him anything, he could tell me anything." (Res 18)*

Another respondent recounted how she and her daughter, as a result of being good friends, were able to discuss personal and intimate issues:

> *"We talk until 3 or 4 in the morning. We have gone through an awful lot. I suppose we have gone deeper until we have almost gone too deep. We talk about everything, adoption, separation, and we still talk." (Res 13)*

And another respondent described how she realised she could never replace her son's adoptive mother. She was very content to have another type of relationship:

> *"It is going well. Absolutely. I mean I certainly would not take over and try and step in and act as his mother, and in actual fact as it turns out now he and I are the best of friends. We talk about everything." (Res 12)*

The development of these friendships involved both losses and gains for the mothers and they also depended on an acceptance by the mothers of what the adoptee was willing or able to offer.

Three respondents gave accounts of how their own wish was for a more intense or frequent relationship with their child, but they realised that this was more than their child had to offer.

One respondent, who had a patterned and predictable structure to her relationship, who had met the adoptive parents and whose other children have a good relationship with the adoptee, described the large gaps which still existed for her:

> "But I'd say we still haven't got to know each other that well, we are still strangers in lots of ways. In the space of three years, only seven meetings or so." (Res 11)

This respondent expressed her sadness that she and her child were not closer, but also noted that for her adopted daughter the level and depth of contact seemed to be satisfactory. She realised that in order for the relationship to continue to work, it was necessary for her to be realistic about what her daughter had to offer to the relationship.

Another respondent who was five years post-reunion described how, in the beginning, she wanted her child to be fully incorporated into her family:

> "He thought he would find me and instead he found a whole family that loved him to bits and that included my mother, his father's mam and dad, uncles that were interested, and they all sent him birthday cards." (Res 9)

This respondent described what happened after she and her son had been in contact for a year:

> "He began taking big steps back, he didn't contact me and I would ring him and he would be chatting as if nothing had happened. He would come and see us but the time was getting longer and longer between visits." (Res 9)

She finally realised:

"It was me being too overpowering to him . . . it was very overwhelming for him." (Res 9)

It took time before she eventually came to understand how the role she expected her child to fill was not possible for him. Now five years later she says:

"The thing I had to do was calm down, and try and get this relationship at a right level rather than this big thing. It is a lovely relationship we have now, but it has taken five years really that we are now all nice and calm." (Res 9)

All of the respondents in this category realised that the reunion was a meeting between two adults who were virtual strangers and that any relationship had to begin from that basis. Hence it was necessary to bracket the "mothering" role and to adopt a role as friend or confidant and to have realistic expectations of how the relationship could develop.

Acceptance of the Child's Adoptive Status

The relationship was working well for respondents who appeared to have come to terms with the adoptive status of their child. Through accepting this status, they recognised that their child was part of another family and had strong links and ties to their adoptive parents. Seven of the ten respondents had met the adoptive parents and one was in regular correspondence. The other three respondents had expressed a wish to meet the adoptive parents and were willing to do so when the time was right for all parties involved.

Respondents described their acceptance of their child's adoptive status in different ways. For two respondents it was an appreciation of the care their child had received:

"After all she was the person who was there for him, the person who fed him, and I would never want him to turn his back on her in any shape or form." (Res 10)

"But I mean you couldn't meet a nicer woman, and that alone, the satisfaction of that alone, that he was very well cared for and very well loved by them." (Res 12)

This respondent went on to recount how she communicated her appreciation and acceptance to her son's adoptive mother:

"I said to her that I really admire her because he has really turned out marvellous, and he is a credit to her, and I told her that. I acknowledged the fact that he is my birth son but she raised him, and I certainly don't deny her that credit." (Res 12)

Two respondents expressed their gratitude for what the adoptive parents had done:

"There are so many stories that I had heard about adopted children and I was wondering if she had gone to the wrong hands. But I am so delighted today. I have a lot to be thankful for to those people, her adopted parents, and at the end of the day they are her parents." (Res 11)

"I felt I could not have done as good a job as what her adoptive parents did on her, she is beautiful." (Res 7)

For four respondents a relationship had developed with the adoptive parents post-reunion, particularly with the adoptive mother. This relationship appeared to enhance the relationship between the respondent and the adoptee.

Two respondents gave details of how they felt their presence in the life of their child was accepted by the adoptive parents. This was important to them particularly around occasions which were identified as important milestones:

"And we all went down for his 21st . . . and we got a photo of the three of us (son and two mothers). She always gave him the support and she always encouraged him when he wanted to look for me and I think that made it a lot easier on me as well." (Res 12)

> *"And her father said, 'You know we are having a party for her 21st and we would be delighted if you would come'. So we went and it was great and we actually stayed with them, with her mother and father, so it was great." (Res 13)*

Relationships with Other Children Born to the Respondents

A friendly and accepting relationship between the adopted child and other children born to the respondents appeared to be another factor which added to a positive relationship between the respondents and the adoptee. Eight of the ten respondents whose relationships with their children were working well had had other children since placing their first-born for adoption. None of the eight mothers had told their other children about their child who had been adopted until contact with their child had been re-established. The mothers had been nervous about communicating such emotional and traumatic news, but as it turned out they need not have worried:

> *"My daughter, she was over the moon, delighted, and the others put their arms around me and hugged me, and were so thrilled . . ." (Res 11)*

> *"Oh I just talked to my family about it and they were very happy for me, and they were saying 'now we have a brother' and they were very happy about it." (Res 17)*

Relationships between the adoptees and those who had not been adopted developed in different ways. In one instance where at time of interview a meeting had not yet been possible there was regular and frequent communication:

> *"Every time there is a birthday, they all get birthday cards from her and from her children." (Res 5)*

In the six instances where the adoptees and the other children born to the respondents had met, relationships had developed and they had become friends:

"They (my son and daughter) met him and they get on ex-tremely well, they go off together and they go up town together . . . so it all gelled." (Res 12)

Respondents described how it had always been their wish that all of their children could, somehow, be together:

"The first weekend she came down we went for a spin and the three of them were playing football together. I was sitting on this little mound and I had tears running down my eyes and I was thinking, 'God the three of them are really together' . . . it was just the four of us and it was a lovely feeling, it was really a lovely feeling." (Res 7)

"And then she came down here and that was a very big step. It was just brilliant seeing the three of them together, it was great. They get on just brilliantly." (Res 13)

The development of friendships and good relationships between the adoptees and the children who had not been adopted was important to the respondents. It also appeared to help solidify the relationship between the respondents and the children they had relinquished.

Relationships Unsatisfactory

In six cases, respondents reported that their relationship with their child was not going well and specified the kinds of difficulties they were experiencing. In two instances contact had been initiated by the mother and in four instances by the adoptee (Table 6.1). In three cases the respondents were one year post-reunion, one respondent was two years post-reunion and in the other two cases the respondents were four and five and years post-reunion respectively (Table 6.2).

In analysing the data, the factors which emerged as militating against establishing and maintaining a satisfactory relationship post-reunion were:

- Haphazard and erratic contact
- Frequency and nature of contact unsatisfactory
- Unrealistic expectations
- Power imbalance within the relationship.

Haphazard and Erratic Contact Pattern

The absence within the relationship of a patterned and predictable contact structure was a key factor for the six respondents whose relationships were not working well. As a result of there being no negotiated agreement as to how the relationship would be conducted, the respondents were unable to rely on the norms they might have used:

> *"I sent a card and there was no acknowledgement . . . and then he went on his holidays and he sent a card. And then Christmas came and went (with no contact) and I thought now that's that." (Res 3)*

Erratic and unpredictable contact patterns left no room for respondents to be sure what really was on offer as a relationship:

> *"But he might not contact me for six months, he might not contact me for a year." (Res 15)*

> *"We kind of stop start — she might be all over me, and then I might not hear anything, and then everything is going grand and she says she will ring next week and I might not hear from her for months." (Res 1)*

In one instance the relationship appeared to be progressing well for a period, but as the respondent began to rely on what would happen next things changed:

> *"It happened there at Christmas, he said, 'I'll be down for Christmas, I'll be down for New Year'. I really had my heart set on that but he didn't come down and there was no explanation why." (Res 2)*

This respondent went on to describe the effect of such unpredictable behaviour:

> *"I think that was hardest of all. I think if a child is going to make no contact at all at least give the mother an explanation why, they deserve that much." (Res 2)*

Not knowing how or when their child would contact caused emotional turmoil for these mothers. They were unable to allow themselves to have confidence and trust in the relationship as there was no way to predict if the relationship was going to continue.

Frequency and Type of Contact Unsatisfactory

In order to establish and develop some depth to a relationship it is necessary to have a level of contact between the individuals involved which will facilitate this outcome. Five respondents attributed some of the problems they perceived in their relationships as being related to the frequency and nature of contact. Three respondents whose relationships were not functioning well identified how in conjunction with the unpredictable patterns that were present in their relationships, the actual frequency with which their children were prepared to meet them led to difficulties in achieving closeness:

One respondent stated:

> *"Well I have had only one meeting since the reunion, there was 11 months between the reunion and the next meeting." (Res 3)*

When reflecting on how her relationship was progressing another respondent stated:

> *"I wouldn't say it is going anywhere. He will ring me and I will meet him. I think the couple of times that I have met him it has been too short to get into any depth of knowing what he is about. I think it is a very cursory way of meeting and knowing somebody." (Res 15)*

One respondent recounted how she believed her child was resisting having a close one-to-one relationship with her:

> *"She would come here on a few occasions, herself and the boy-friend, and herself and another one of her family, a sister. We don't get to talk that much." (Res 16)*

In contrast to the above, in some relationships *too much* unpredictable and unregulated contact with the child led to problems. One respondent described how she felt that the relationship was too casual and without respect for her privacy. Her son called round to see her very frequently but always without any warning that he would be coming. She had requested that he phone ahead when he was going to "pop in" but this did not happen. Her own conclusion was:

> *"And I knew myself that he would be just killing time, his friend wouldn't be home from work, so he would come in here killing a few hours." (Res 14)*

It was the respondent's belief that as a result of the relationship not having a solid foundation it had faltered. The last contact went thus:

> *"We had a chat on the phone, but he never said he was going to call out and I never said do you want to call out. I decided to leave it to him. So that was three months ago and I haven't heard from him since." (Res 14)*

Power Imbalance within the Relationship

The existence of a power imbalance within the relationship between mother and child appeared to be a major impediment to building a trusting and mutually satisfactory and lasting relationship. Six respondents expressed feelings of disempowerment which largely appeared to be derived from their belief that, in relinquishing their child they had also relinquished their rights to be able to express their wishes and needs within the developing relationship post-reunion. In one instance where the relationship was not developing as the respondent wished, she stated that she was unsure of her own "rights" in regard to initiating contact:

> *"So when he made no contact, I didn't feel I should make a move. It was up to him to make the decisions." (Res 2)*

Not only did this respondent feel that she had no entitlement to make any demands within the relationship, but her own confidence and self esteem were affected by the way things had progressed. *She* believed that her son was conducting the relationship in a certain way because he was not satisfied or happy with the person he had found through reunion:

> *"But what you are actually feeling is, 'what did you do, what did you say, you've said something, he has found some fault in you and that is reeling around in your head for months and months'." (Res 2)*

Another respondent also presumed she had no entitlement to information which would enable her to contact her child:

> *"I didn't have a telephone number for him, because I thought he didn't have a telephone in the house, but as it transpired he did, but he probably didn't want me to have it." (Res 15)*

And another respondent described how the power balance within this very important relationship was quite askew compared to other relationships in her life:

> *"I'm a lot straighter with other people about how I feel about things, but I'm not with her and I feel like I'm walking on egg shells with her, so I am not happy." (Res 1)*

These respondents did not feel they could or should exercise control over the direction or type of relationship that was to develop. It was left to the child to decide the boundaries and contact arrangements. As a result, in some cases there was a total asymmetry of power.

Unrealistic Expectations

If the respondents had set expectations that were not met, or which could potentially never be met, there were difficulties and conflicts in the relationships. Respondents who were unable to see beyond their own wishes and needs were disappointed and dissatisfied with how the relationship developed. One respondent described how, especially in the beginning, her expectations were that the years since relinquishment could be obliterated:

> *"I assumed that the minute I saw him that would be it, 18 years would be gone out the window." (Res 14)*

Another respondent had developed expectations around what her child would do once their relationship had been established:

> *"I think I had these expectations that everything was going to be hunky dory, I was thinking he might move down here eventually." (Res 2)*

And another respondent found it hard to come to terms with the kind of relationship her daughter was offering:

> *"You would like a mother and daughter relationship, and I don't think that is there." (Res 16)*

Unlike the respondents whose relationships were working well, these respondents displayed an inability to recognise that as a result of being adopted their child was most likely bonded and attached to another family to whom they had commitments and loyalties. The respondents were seeking a commitment from the relationship which did not appear to be available.

Relationship Ceased

At time of interview two respondents were no longer in contact with their child. In both instances it was the child who had initiated contact (Table 6.1). One respondent was one year post-reunion and the other was six years post-reunion (Table 6.2). The manner in which contact ceased was different for each respondent.

For the respondent who was one year post-reunion, contact had been discontinued by the child immediately after the reunion meeting. This respondent stated that she had no idea or information as to why her child chose to sever the contact that he had initiated. She described how she thought her reunion meeting had gone well and how she had been given reason to expect that contact would continue:

> *". . . and the last thing he said (at the end of the reunion meeting) was, 'I hope it won't be long until we meet again'." (Res 8)*

When her son did not contact her again, the respondent gave details about her efforts to find out why:

> *"The social worker wrote a few times on my behalf, and there has been no correspondence. I sent him a Christmas card and there was no correspondence." (Res 8)*

For this respondent, having no explanation as to why her son had chosen not to remain in contact had been extremely difficult and distressing. She described feeling "lonely and pained" as she wondered about him and his whereabouts. She was back to speculating:

> *"Because you keep thinking every day, is he dead or alive?"*
> *(Res 8)*

In many ways this respondent was even more powerless than she had been prior to reunion. Her fantasies about meeting the child she relinquished had become reality, but since contact was severed she now had a new set of questions about the ongoing welfare of her child. The reunion had offered little in the way of relief or closure.

For the second respondent who at time of interview was six years post-reunion the situation developed in a different way.

> *"She used to come out fairly regularly, about every six weeks.*
> *Then she would say she was going to come but she wouldn't*
> *turn up. I rang her about two years ago, on New Year's night,*
> *and she said she would ring me again in a week, and that was*
> *the last I heard from her." (Res 6)*

This respondent has never been able to establish a reason as to why her child had severed contact. Like the previous respondent she found it distressing and painful that contact had been severed. She stated that she felt it to be even more painful than before since it was now her daughter who was choosing not to keep in touch.

Chapter 7

REFLECTIONS ON REUNION

"At the end of the day you want to be their Mam, because that is what you are." (Res 18)

Respondents in this study were asked to reflect overall on the outcome of their reunions. In doing so they highlighted the complexity of feelings and emotions they experienced as a result of being reconnected with their child. They reflected on the benefits which they believed had accrued to them as a result of reunion, and also how reunion had brought renewed sadness.

All of the respondents were clear and unequivocal about the fact that they were glad they had met with their child. Regardless of whether their reunion had worked out as they had wished or whether they were still in contact with their child, all of the 18 respondents expressed satisfaction that they had gone through with the reunion.

For natural mothers, the most frequently mentioned benefits of reunion were:

- Knowing their child was alive and well

- Being able to give their child the true account of their adoption history

- Increased self-confidence and self-belief

- Easing of guilt.

Benefits of Reunion

Knowing Their Child Was Alive and Well

Respondents recounted how, in the years prior to reunion, not having any information had been very difficult for them. They described the reality of not knowing as "appalling" and "awful". However, once letters and photographs had been exchanged and the reunion meetings had taken place, respondents had, after periods of 16 to 40 years, finally been able to confirm for themselves that their child was alive and well. They now knew that their child continued to exist even if their name had been changed and they were living under a different identity.

One respondent described what she thought to herself as she looked at photographs of her son which had been sent to her prior to reunion:

"My God, he really does exist." (Res 3)

Other respondents described how the knowledge and information they gained about their child at the reunion brought relief:

"On Christmas morning I used to sit and think, what is she doing, where is she? It was a different Christmas this year, there wasn't a void in it."(Res 7)

"Just knowing that he is ok, I am happy with that." (Res 2)

Respondents whose reunions had not worked out to their satisfaction were also positive. For the respondent whose son had severed contact after the first meeting, there was still a positive aspect to the meeting:

"I am delighted that I did see him." (Res 8)

One respondent, despite the fact that she perceived her relationship was unsatisfactory, described how it had been beneficial for her to meet her child:

> *"I feel more fulfilled, that day was probably the best thing that ever happened to me in my life, that I met him." (Res 15)*

An Opportunity to Give the True Account of Adoption

All the respondents described how, in the years post-relinquishment, they had always wished they would be given an opportunity to be able to explain to their child the true circumstances which led to their being placed for adoption. Throughout the years during which their child had been absent, they had no way of knowing what "story" had been told about the reasons for relinquishment. The reunion meeting gave the respondents the chance to tell what happened from their own very personal perspective. One respondent described how she had always felt it would be her responsibility as a mother who had given birth to do this:

> *"I filled in some of the jigsaw for him, I fulfilled my duty to him." (Res 3)*

Two other respondents welcomed the opportunity to give the facts of what happened:

> *"He had a lot of questions to ask and they had to be answered and answered truthfully." (Res 10)*

> *"I have met my own flesh and blood and I have told him what he was like as a baby, and things that I wanted to tell him." (Res 17)*

A face-to-face reunion meeting with their child served many purposes for these respondents, but having the occasion to be honest and truthful with their child about the past was one of the most important.

Increased Self-confidence and Self-belief

All of the respondents described how their own self-confidence, self-worth and self-belief were enhanced as a result of meeting their child. The shame and stigma which had been attached to having a child outside marriage had remained with them through the years, but reunion offered some release:

"I felt my personality changed after I met my son, my outlook now was, 'I don't give a damn what people say or think anymore'. I felt I was hidden under a cloud for those 20 years, I felt inferior because I had signed him away and because I had had him out of wedlock, and I lacked a lot of confidence because of that." (Res 12)

Surviving the trauma and ordeal of adoption was liberating:

"It has changed my life, changed my perception on life, changed the way I feel about myself. And I am very proud that I actually got through it, very, very proud that I actually got through the adoption and the 18 years." (Res 14)

And to begin to believe that what they had done was not evil was important:

"I am more secure than what I was, am more happy in myself than what I was. I know I am not the bad egg like I was told I was." (Res 2)

The final breaking of the silence around their identity as the mother of this adopted child made them feel confident and self-assured:

"I wanted to tell the whole world because it wasn't a secret any longer. It was a secret, a heartbreaking secret for so long." (Res 14)

And for some, the release from having to repress their emotions was important:

"After meeting him I am a very happy person. I am so happy I cannot express it to you. It has made me complete." (Res 17)

Easing of Guilt

As discussed earlier, parting with their child had left all of the respondents with overwhelming feelings of guilt and self-reproach which had not abated over time. The event of reunion and the subsequent development of a relationship with their child brought relief for the respondents, albeit that in most cases the relief was only partial:

> *"You carry this awful guilt around with you, you carry it like you are carrying a suitcase full of lead, and it never goes, it just gets easier, but it never goes." (Res 14)*

Only one respondent believed that her sense of guilt had abated completely:

> *"I don't blame myself anymore, I have no guilt anymore. I was feeling guilty until I knew she was alive and well." (Res 5)*

Sadness in the Aftermath of Reunion

Despite whether they identified their relationships as satisfactory or unsatisfactory, all of the respondents in this study identified how for them a very real and ongoing sadness emerged for them in the aftermath of reunion. They described, how, despite the happiness they experienced as a result of meeting their child, they also felt a deep loss for what they had missed and continued to yearn for what might have been.

Respondents described how, as they got to know their child better, their sense of loss magnified:

> *"The fact that he is a carbon copy of myself, personality and everything was sort of, look at the loss, look at what I have missed out on." (Res 18)*

They identified how they went through lonesome periods after the reunion, especially if they did not ever have the opportunity to have another child.

There was sadness too about the *kind* of relationship which had been lost:

> *"We are more or less friends really, rather than mother and daughter. Sometimes that hurts, that hurts, you know it hurts me." (Res 7)*

> *"Because no matter how much you say, 'OK this doesn't matter to you or that doesn't matter to you', it does matter to you, it matters that you are his mother and that you are not his birth mother as they want to call you." (Res 18)*

And yet another two respondents identified how, in the aftermath of reunion, they realised that the life-long gain for adoptive parents had been at the expense of their sadness and loss:

> *"They are her parents and always will be and I am more or less like a stranger to her." (Res 11)*

> *"I mean what I find personally difficult is that she has a life and a family that is not us, no matter how close we get." (Res 13)*

For the respondents whose children's names had been changed at adoption there was great sadness. The realisation of the degree to which they had been disempowered became more intense as they had to adjust to getting to know their child under a different identity:

> *"It was very hard, I just cried over it. It just took away from me the bit of dignity I had about the child." (Res 16)*

> *"I thought that when I had christened him, which was a nice name, I presumed he would keep it, I mean it was only me thinking." (Res 15)*

> *"That was hard, it was hard for quite a long time, I know it is a very minor thing, but for 20 years you are thinking of them with that name." (Res 13)*

It was painful for the respondents to reflect how things could have been different in the more liberal climate of today where lone parenthood is more acceptable:

> *"How sad it was to have missed her all those years. I just wish things could have been different and if it had been a few years down the line it would have been different." (Res 16)*

> *"Even my brother's girlfriend now, she had a baby, and I often see it and it is heartbreaking." (Res 8)*

Respondents identified how coming to a realisation that the conflict that existed between their own needs and the reality of what the new relationship might have to offer was distressing:

> *"It is like when I met her it was this tall blond slim young woman and I had left a six-day-old baby and there is more of me needed to hold the baby than the relationship with this young woman." (Res 1)*

> *"But the big thing about adopted kids is that we need them more than they need us. I think personally because we have lost something so deep, but they don't necessarily feel that because they have a mam and dad, and my need for him was an awful lot more than his need for me." (Res 9)*

For these mothers there was a realisation that whereas reunion brought some closure and emotional relief, ultimately what had been lost could never be retrieved.

Summary

In the period immediately after the reunion meeting the respondents were again thrown into emotional turmoil as they anticipated whether a relationship would develop. In cases where relationships developed there was trust and a growing confidence in the relationship. The respondents believed they had a basis on which to have a satisfactory relationship. In cases where relationships were not working satisfactorily, an inability to place trust in the relationship due to the absence of anchoring factors in the relationship appeared to be the key reason for it not developing well. All of the respondents were happy to have met their child, but meeting their child as an adult brought up new feelings of guilt and sadness which mothers had not anticipated. The emotional consequences of relinquishment carried on in the aftermath of reunion.

Chapter 8

DISCUSSION (1):
PREGNANCY AND RELINQUISHMENT —
DISEMPOWERED MOTHERS

In Chapters 4–7 the views and narratives of the respondents in relation to their experience of pregnancy, adoption and reunion were presented in their own words. Their personal and individual reflections on how adoption and reunion had impacted on their lives were also recounted. The aim of this and the next two chapters is to interpret and contextualise those experiences.

Non-marital Pregnancy as a Crisis

In Ireland in 1954, non-marital births represented 2.09 per cent of all births, in 1967 this figure was 2.02 per cent and in 1974 it had increased to 3.35 per cent.[1] The fact that non-marital pregnancy and the existence of an "illegitimate" child were perceived as problems had its roots in a number of beliefs which prevailed during the period when these mothers gave birth. Society's attitudes to sexual activity were shaped by Catholic social teachings which deemed sexual intercourse outside marriage to be sinful and immoral. Much of what was written and spoken about in relation to sexuality during the nineteenth and twentieth centuries was dominated by the teachings and ethos of the Catholic Church. The Catholic Church provided the religious moral discourse through its control of schools and via its influence in many state institu-

---

[1] *Sources*: Statistical Abstracts (various years) Central Statistics Office, Dublin.

tions (Inglis, 1987; Cooney, 1999). The beliefs which permeated Irish society as a result of the church's teaching was that sex should be confined to marriage and by implication pregnancy and the birth of children belonged within marriage. In 1974 for example, a national survey found that 71 per cent of the Catholic respondents thought that a man and a woman having sexual relations before marriage was always wrong. This in effect represented most of the population, since 96 per cent of the Republic of Ireland's population was Catholic (Inglis, 1987).

Catholic moral theology was particularly strict in relation to women and sexuality. In the game of love and lust, it was the task of single women to remain chaste and virginal, and certainly not to become pregnant. It was the task of mothers to make sure they instilled a sense of modesty in their daughters and that they did not lose it through having sexual relations (Inglis, 1987). These teachings of the Church were enforced within society, within schools and within families through a series of strategies based on creating shame, embarrassment and guilt. All of these strategies were reinforced if a woman became pregnant outside marriage. For example, one of the respondents in this study believed she could not tell her twin brother she was pregnant because she believed he would be expelled from the seminary where he was studying for the priesthood. Batts (1994), who lived through being pregnant in the 1960s, further describes how such strategies worked:

> . . . being pregnant and unmarried in Ireland in the sixties was the most horrific experience imaginable . . . this was Ireland at the time when sins against the sixth commandment were considered very serious indeed and everything relating to sexual intercourse and pregnancy was regarded as the fault of the woman alone.

As a result of having had sex outside marriage, therefore, the women in this study had offended the established moral code which resulted in their being shamed and often ostracised.

This harsh and unforgiving attitude was not just a societal response; in many instances it was the response within families. For the majority (14) of the respondents in this study who told family members, the reaction they received to the announcement of their pregnancy was one of disappointment, shock and anger. The prevailing belief at the time was that the best preparation for a happy Catholic marriage was to be chaste, temperate, and charitable, to pray to God for guidance in choosing a partner, and to ask the advice of parents and a confessor (Cooney, 1999). If, as was the case for the women in this study, a daughter was pregnant outside marriage, the accepted moral code had been broken as she was no longer chaste and virginal. Parents were often angry that their daughter had disobeyed their instructions not to engage in sexual intercourse before marriage. The fears of parents about the stigma which could attach to a family as a result of having an illegitimate child born to one of their children were very real and genuine. It was a difficult time also for parents. It is noteworthy that such negative and unforgiving attitudes by parents and family to the disclosure of non-marital pregnancy have also been recorded by research in other countries. In Scotland, Bouchier et al. (1991) found that "families themselves were critical, often against a strong moral or religious background, and some used physical or uncontrolled verbal abuse". For the women in this study, the consequences and price of such fear, shame and embarrassment on behalf of their parents were high. It must have been difficult for them to discover that when they most needed support, it was not available from where it might have been expected.

The majority (14) of the pregnancies in this research took place in the 1970s. What these reactions to non-marital pregnancy demonstrate is that despite the winds of change in Ireland in the 1970s (the founding of the Women's Movement in 1971, the introduction of Unmarried Mothers Allowance in 1973, the introduction of equality legislation in 1976) to become pregnant outside marriage remained problematised and highly stigmatised. The discourse of sexuality in Ireland was still silenced. Sex was equated with procreation and legitimised only in the context of marriage. A person's standing, especially in a small rural community, derived from their adherence to the community's social and moral norms.

As a result of all of these factors, the event of non-marital pregnancy was almost invariably a crisis.

Adoption as a Solution to Crisis Pregnancy

For a large proportion of women who became pregnant outside
marriage the solution to the crisis was to relinquish their child
through adoption. In 1954, 67.8 per cent of non-marital births resulted in adoption; in 1964 this figure had increased to 77.6 per
cent and in 1974 it was still a large percentage at 57.4 per cent. At
no time during the 20-year period from 1954 to 1974 did the percentage represent less than 50 per cent of all births outside marriage. In 1967 it reached an all-time high of 96.9 per cent.[2]

Table 8.1: Adoption Trends, 1954–1974

Year	Non-marital Births as % of Total Births	Adoptions as % of Non-marital Births
1954	2.09%	67.8%
1964	2.02%	77.6%
1974	3.35%	57.4%

As these statistics demonstrate, for women in Ireland during the
1950s, 1960s and continuing into the 1970s, the normal or most
common response to a crisis pregnancy was, without question,
relinquishment through adoption. The fact that adoption was, at
the time, the most common solution to non-marital pregnancy
appears to have been as a result of a number of different factors.

One significant factor in adoption being considered as the solution to non-marital pregnancy was the prevailing belief that a
woman who had become pregnant outside marriage had now
taken on the status of having a "spoiled identity". As demonstrated in this and in previous research and literature this "spoiled
identity" of the woman who was pregnant outside marriage had to
be managed and effectively silenced. This was most often done by

---

[2] Annual Report, Adoption Board, 1999, Dublin.

removing the mother to another place where she was not known (Bouchier et al., 1991; Howe et al., 1992) and where the process of hiding and silencing the pregnancy could be undertaken.

For the majority of mothers in this study, leaving home meant having to find refuge in a place where the secrecy about their pregnancy could be maintained. Five of the respondents in this study went to the homes of relatives or friends who were willing to accommodate them throughout the duration of the pregnancy. These relatives and friends lived in different parts of the country from where the pregnant women's family were, and as part of the contract of offering refuge, agreed to collude in the process of keeping the non-marital pregnancy a secret. This collusion ensured that the stigma attached to the "condition" of the women did not, at the very least, attach to their families of origin. For the women themselves there was some relief from the disgrace which would most likely have been their lot in the locality from which they came. Although at the time the women may have been grateful for the accommodation offered, the facts were that through such support there was further collusion in silencing the pregnancy. Respondents reported how their relatives and friends made it clear that they believed a child should have two parents. The pressure which these women felt to relinquish their child for adoption had begun even before the child was born.

Six of the respondents sought refuge in Mother and Baby Homes. These institutions and the services they offered were, as outlined earlier, an official state response to the "problem" of women who became pregnant outside marriage. Accommodation was offered throughout the pregnancy and in the aftermath. State grants which were not available to women living in the community, were paid from the County Councils of the counties from which the women originated to pay for their upkeep at the Home. Despite the fact that these Homes were supported through the state, the conditions and services which were offered to the women were often very poor. None of the respondents in this study, for example, recalled having been given the opportunity to discuss what choices they might have had or what assistance might be available to them if they wanted to keep their child. The atmosphere and ethos of these Homes was one of secrecy, shame and punishment. The collusion with the silencing of the pregnancy which had been instigated by virtue of the women seeking refuge was continued and supported. The expectation was that once the pregnancy was over the child would disappear. The message which the women in this study received from the authorities in these state-sponsored Homes was that adoption was really the only option for a single pregnant woman and her impending illegitimate child.

In Ireland in the early 1970s a system of "family placement" was introduced for single pregnant women. Host families who were willing to offer accommodation to single pregnant women for the duration of their pregnancy were recruited through voluntary organisations and clergy.[3] The accommodation offered to the woman in question was always out of her own community where secrecy and anonymity were guaranteed. Five of the respondents in this study availed of such accommodation during their pregnancies. Whereas for the time such arrangements were considered to be quite progressive, the accounts of three of the respondents in this study indicate that for them, this system compounded their lack of choice in relation to their child. None of the respondents remembered receiving any counselling from the agencies that had placed them during their time with these families. Whereas families may have believed they were offering support and confidentiality to single pregnant women who were their guests, to the respondents in this study it appeared that the families with whom they were staying were colluding in the secrecy and silencing about the pregnancy. They also gained the impression from their hosts that it was expected that the child of their guest would be relinquished for adoption. Whereas this system offered respite from the stigma which attached to being in their own communities, at least for the

---

[3] ALLY, which operated from the Dominican Priory in Dublin, was one such organisation which located family placements. A number of the voluntary adoption agencies also arranged family placements for the women who presented to them during pregnancy requesting assistance.

respondents in this study it did little to empower the women in relation to having any choices about their child.

Another factor which appeared to have the effect of exerting
pressure on women to make a decision in favour of adoption was
the lack of state support for lone parenthood. The official ethos of
the state in relation to what constitutes a family was not supportive of the concept of a single parent being recognised as a family.
In Ireland, the belief as to what constitutes the *normal* family
structure is protected in the Constitution. For instance, Article 41.1
of the Constitution states:

> The state recognises the Family as the natural primary and
> fundamental unit group of Society, and as a moral institu-
> tion, possessing inalienable and imprescriptible rights, an-
> tecedent and superior to all positive law.

The Constitution further goes on to protect mothers within families through Article 41.2:

> In particular, the State recognises that by her life within the
> home, woman gives to the State a support without which
> the common good cannot be achieved.

Both of these Articles from the Irish Constitution seem to imply
that motherhood in Ireland is defined within the institution of
marriage. Such descriptions as to how motherhood should be defined gave further credence to the belief that the reproduction of
children belonged within the institution of marriage and not with
single pregnant women.

In conjunction with the ethos of the state being experienced as
discriminatory, the reality of the economic position of unmarried
mothers in Ireland up to 1973 was extremely difficult. Writing in
1973, Maher suggested that "keeping your baby is difficult in Ireland on the small welfare provision made for unmarried mothers". In the event of their not being able to work, the state welfare
payments of Home Assistance and Children's Allowance were
insufficient to provide an unmarried mother and her child with
any decent standard of living. Living accommodation for single

mothers with a child was difficult to find and landlords in many cases actually refused to rent to single women with children (Richards, 1981; Richards, 1998). The introduction of the Unmarried Mothers Allowance in 1973 is credited with providing some choice to women about keeping their babies as opposed to relinquishing them for adoption (McCashin, 1996; McMahon et al., 1998; Richards, 1998). But in order for the existence of such a payment to be become known to a young unmarried mother, the state and helping agencies needed to be proactive in informing them of its existence. None of the respondents in this study who had their children subsequent to the introduction of Unmarried Mothers Allowance remember being offered any information about their entitlement to this allowance. Through this lack of knowledge the mothers were further disempowered in relation to the decision about adoption as they believed they could not support their child alone.

Beliefs about the ideal family of two married parents being essential for the moral and physical welfare of a child were also a factor in adoption becoming the solution to the problem of non-marital children (Inglis, 1984). The widely held view was that the security which a married couple could provide was not available from a mother who was not wed (Triseliotis, Shireman and Hundleby, 1997). These beliefs were current in Irish society and permeated the ethos of adoption agencies and Mother and Baby Homes from which single pregnant women sought assistance. Unlike the status of "illegitimacy" the status of "adopted" did not carry a stigma; rather it was regarded as a status which had "saved" the child from the stigma of illegitimacy. By implication the child's mother was also saved from the stigma and shame of being an unmarried mother (Solinger, 1994; Triseliotis, Shireman and Hundleby, 1997). The majority (17) of the mothers in this study stated that they did not remember any options other than adoption being discussed with them in any meaningful way by the social workers with whom they were in contact. It appeared that the ethos, philosophy and practice of agencies was to promote adoption as the best possible choice and solution for a single pregnant woman.

This absence of support from parents, relatives, helping agencies and the state was a crucial factor for the respondents in this study in having to accept the inevitability of adoption. Winkler and Van Keppel (1984) also record in the findings of their study that women in Australia felt they had "little choice" but to surrender their child due of the lack of support they received from parents and helping agencies. Condon (1986) concluded that the women in her study believed they were "forced" to part with their child due to a lack of support. Sullivan and Groden (1995) also cited "pressure from parents" as being a factor for relinquishing mothers in having to choose adoption. Sullivan and Groden (1995) also state that for most mothers in their study "keeping their babies was not an option". Almost 90 per cent of them said they had no other choice at the time. Lack of finance, marital status, social pressure combined to preclude the option of keeping their babies. Silverman et al. (1988) also found that "many birth parents felt pressured by adoption agencies to surrender, they felt coerced into agreeing they could/should not keep the baby". Through the application of many or all of these pressures the single pregnant women in this study were disempowered in relation to their choices about the future for their child. Their ability to act voluntarily was suspended or removed. Although writing about the situation in the United States, Solinger's (1984) summary of why adoption in the 1950s and 1960s was seen as a solution to non-marital pregnancy could equally have been applied in Ireland:

> Through adoption then, the unwed mother could put the mistakes, both the baby and the proof of non-marital sexual experience, behind her. Her parents were not stuck with a ruined daughter and a ruined grandchild for life. And the baby could be brought up in a normative family, by a couple prejudged to possess all the attributes and resources necessary for successful parenthood.

A very different attitude on the part of parents to crisis pregnancy has been highlighted in recent studies. In the findings of their study on crisis pregnancies, Mahon et al. (1998) point out that for women who felt they could choose lone parenthood, parents emerged as the key sources of support. For example, "they helped women adjust to the prospect of motherhood, provided accommodation and promised child care which in turn relieved financial pressures, and provided them with important emotional and psychological support". McCashin (1996) records in his study that young women who became pregnant outside marriage received a high degree of support from significant others, especially their parents. While fearful and apprehensive, they were not panic-stricken and they believed themselves to have certain choices which included the possibility of keeping their child.

In the Mahon et al. (1998) study it was also found that women with crisis pregnancies were typically younger and single without a stable relationship. They had become pregnant in a social and personal context in which continuing the pregnancy was problematic. Despite these problems, however, like the women in McCashin's (1996) study, they viewed their situation from the perspective of having a choice, including the choice of adoption or termination.

The situation of the respondents in both of these recent studies contrasts starkly with the experiences outlined by respondents in this research, all eighteen of whom described being panic-stricken on learning of their pregnancy. If at the time of pregnancy, the parents of the young women in this study had responded differently by, for example, offering to integrate the mother and her child into the extended family, it is possible that they might not have had to give up their children.

Silencing Motherhood

In his analysis of the presentation of self in everyday life, Goffman (1959) describes how people are constantly employed in "preventative practices" to avoid embarrassment. He suggests that if these preventative practices are not sufficient, "corrective practices" are employed to compensate for discrediting occurrences that have not been successfully avoided. These protective and corrective practices comprise the techniques employed to safeguard the impression fostered by individuals during their presence before others especially within families, communities and neighbourhoods.

For mothers in this and other studies, the key corrective practice employed by those who were aware of the relinquishment was the imposition of a total silence about what had happened. Howe et al. (1992) suggest that this silence was imposed through the denial of any recognition of the existence of natural mothers:

> . . . she was forgotten, even denied. She was the neglected corner of the adoption triangle. Not until the child started to ask about his or her origins did the mother reappear, but her image was frozen in time. The last occasion she was seen was at the moment of placement.

Logan (1996) found that even when the natural mother went on to marry the father of the child, that silence was still imposed as "husbands were reluctant to open up old wounds". In this present study, once their child had been relinquished respondents were told by parents that "we will never talk about this again". The facts of what had happened were known, but through the imposition of silence the facts were denied. The fear of the stigma that would attach to families and the need to adhere to a strict moral code of an unchanged social order overrode any other considerations. The impression that there had been no pregnancy and that no child existed had to be maintained.

Other corrective practices were also employed. Some of these occurred as a result of the very nature of the closed adoption practices of adoption agencies. After relinquishment, information was rarely given to a relinquishing mother about the whereabouts of her child or indeed about the kind of home in which the child had been placed. The name which had been given by the natural mother to her child at birth was often changed, and this information was often not communicated to the natural mother. In some instances when information was given to adoptive parents, parts of the natural mother's history were suppressed (Farrelly Conway, 1993). As part of the impression management of adoption an attempt was made to write the natural mothers out of the adoption process. Given the shame and disgrace that was heaped upon them as a result of having given birth to an illegitimate child, relinquishing mothers might have been expected to be grateful for these policies, but as Inglis (1984) says, "none was given the choice". What relinquishing mothers were offered was secrecy rather than privacy, a secrecy that was to be damaging and disempowering for many years to come.

In the years following relinquishment, despite what they might otherwise have wished, the mothers themselves were also forced to become part of the silencing process around the existence of their child. They had no option but to employ their own corrective practices. Impression and stigma management were necessary as a woman who became pregnant outside marriage was the subject of considerable prejudice. For the respondents in this study the secret had to be managed. Being obliged, in later years for instance, to plan to attend a hospital where they were not known in order to give birth to what everyone else believed to be their "first" child was distressing and was evidence of the kind of continuing work relinquishing mothers had to engage in to keep their secret safe. Answering simple enquiries from acquaintances and friends such as "How many children do you have?" involved them in a painful denial process about their own reality. In order to survive the pain and sadness involved in the denial of their child, relinquishing mothers often had to develop what Hochschild (1990) describes as a "protective sixth sense", the psychological equivalent of a status shield. Because of the shame and stigma attached to their status, the process of denial became their status shield and using it was how they survived. In the end, they could not even be true to themselves.

Prolonged Experience of Grief

According to Robinson (2000), "the grief of the woman who has lost her child through adoption is a unique experience and differs in fundamental ways from other grief experiences". The respondents in this study all experienced continuing feelings of ongoing grief and sadness which, as found in previous studies (Winkler and Van Keppel, 1984; Cotton and Parish, 1987; Silverman et al., 1988), for large numbers of women were not resolved over time. Robinson (2000) suggests that one of the key reasons for the unresolved nature of the grief of a woman who had to part with her child is that it has never been recognised, it has never become legitimate. It has, as Doka (1989) suggests, been disenfranchised. A significant feature of disenfranchised grief is the absence of rituals, which in their capacity as the mourning activities associated with bereavement, assist the bereaved in their adjustment to loss. These activities and rituals also provide the bereaved with permission and an opportunity to mourn. For the relinquishing mothers in this study, from the very start of their pregnancies, there were no "approving" rituals attached to the announcement of their pregnancy, no celebration about the event of the birth. Where relinquishment was concerned, there were no "mourning" rituals around the loss that had taken place and there was no sympathy or public recognition of the pain of relinquishment. Through the imposition of the silence around the existence of their child, they were denied any opportunity even to begin to resolve their grief. The mothers had no options but to be a part of the collusion to silence the existence of their child and to internalise their intense and distressing grief.

Efforts to Regain Control

The perception of the majority of the respondents in this research was that there was a lack of concern about their ongoing welfare from the agencies through which they placed their children. Their experience was similar to the experience of the relinquishing mothers in the study by Howe et al. (1992) who found that:

> . . . once the decision had been made to surrender the child, many mothers felt that the adoption worker lost all interest in them and concentrated entirely on the baby. The birth mother had produced the baby and once the decision had been made, they were out of the picture and of no further interest.

Although the respondents in this study have no memory of having agency policies explained to them, given the closed system of adoption, it should not have come as a surprise that agencies would have no further service to offer them. This does not account however, for the practice of agencies ignoring the efforts of mothers to have up-to-date information inserted in the file at the agency. As one respondent in this study described, having to engage a solicitor to write on her behalf so that she might get a response was unreasonable and unfair to a woman who was just trying to make sure her child knew she cared. For the mothers who did write to agencies, their belief was that they had made efforts to keep in contact with their child. It is difficult to be able to explain exactly why agencies treated these mothers in such a way. It may be, as suggested by Darling (1974), that the agencies were understaffed, or perhaps they had policies of not offering an ongoing service to relinquishing mothers. Perhaps they had no policies at all, but whatever the reasons, the results of their actions were to further disempower these mothers.

As respondents' accounts demonstrate, some of the mothers did not believe they had any right even to consider taking some control over their situation. It was apparent that they had absorbed and internalised the authoritarian nature of the agency's instructions issued to them upon relinquishment. In one case, a respondent who did not remember the birth, and also did not remember signing the final consent, had a very clear memory of being told, "you are forbidden to ever try to make contact". She, like many of the other respondents who absorbed the ethos of the agency, would never have countenanced approaching an agency to look for information or a possible reunion. It is important to consider that in the instances where the respondents did not feel empowered to begin a search themselves they might never have had the opportunity of reunion if their child had not been willing to initiate contact.

Chapter 9

DISCUSSION (2):
MOTHER AND CHILD REUNITED —
AN EMOTIONALLY CHARGED EXPERIENCE

The mythology of motherhood suggests that the very word "mother" resonates with permanence, intimacy and care. The bonds between a woman and the child she carried within her body seem inviolable (Inglis, 1984). In our culture, the women who bear children generally care for them; to be a mother means to be available for your child in the role of mother and to know what is happening for them. The continuity and expansion of the relationship between mother and child as the child develops is one of our most cherished values (Inglis, 1984). In this context the surrender of a child to strangers through the process of closed adoption seems strange and somewhat incomprehensible. Yet the experience of surrendering her child to strangers about whom she was rarely given any information was the experience of all of the respondents in this study, as it was for the majority of women worldwide who relinquished their children through adoption.

Why Reunions are Happening

Many of the influences and conditions which legitimated the process of closed or stranger adoption have been discussed above and in the literature reviewed for this study. Explaining the relinquishment of children in the context of the prevailing beliefs and customs of the time does not, however, explain the reasons for the increasing number of reunions which are now taking place. In Ireland, these reunions are happening despite the continued existence of closed adoption. The research and literature which has been published on reunions does not specifically address the question of why there has been a growth in adoption reunion. From the findings of this and previous research, however, it is possible to speculate as to why reunions have become part of the adoption process.

From the point of view of natural mothers, the first and most obvious reason why a reunion may be desired is because these mothers have never forgotten their children and in many cases have longed for the day when they could reunite. In the aftermath of relinquishment, the natural mothers' experience was one of profound sadness and guilt about the decision that they had made or been forced to make. In many instances they lived their lives with feelings of unresolved grief which affected their personalities and sense of self in a negative way. The denial of the existence of their child became increasingly difficult for them. Throughout the years when their child was growing up, because they had been given no information, they wondered and worried about whether their child was alive and happy. They had once been a mother to their child and, despite relinquishment, continued to have the concerns and instincts that were attached to being a mother. As their child grew older they yearned for an opportunity to explain the circumstances of relinquishment. These mothers never forgot their children. It was always their hope that at the very least they would be able to establish if their child was alive and well. Their fantasies and desires were that they might have a reunion.

The natural mother's wish to have a reunion was not, however, a sufficient reason for it to happen. They had been disempowered through the adoption process and in many countries continued to be so through the current legislation or lack of legislation.[1] Respondents in this study related the difficulties they en-

---

[1] In England and Wales for example, whereas natural mothers have a right to put their name on the National Contact Register, a search will be undertaken by the

countered as a result of even trying to put information about themselves on file at adoption agencies in the event of their child ever wishing to search for them. Despite these difficulties however, many mothers persisted and managed to get the agencies to acknowledge and agree that if their child ever came looking for them the agency would contact them. As referred to earlier in this study, there are no official statistics available to indicate how many children have come forward and had a reunion with their natural mothers, but the fact that all 13 registered adoption agencies provide this service and are involved in the facilitation of reunions would indicate that reunions are happening reasonably frequently and that there is a demand for the service.

Perhaps the biggest influence in changing attitudes towards closed adoption and the subsequent initiation of reunions has come from the children whom natural mothers had relinquished. Adopted people's desire to know their roots is a universal phenomenon and is part of normal personality development (Sachdev, 1989, quoted in Howe and Feast, 2000). Being adopted marks people out socially as being different, and in a sense as not "normal". Searching is seen as an attempt to account for this difference and establish a more complete social identity (Howe and Feast, 2000). This growing desire of adopted people to know about their origins meant that agencies in many countries, including Ireland, were receiving large numbers of enquires requesting information on birth heritage. Adopted people were also often expressing a desire to meet with birth relatives. The voice and active campaigning of these adults to establish their right to information led, in a number of jurisdictions,[2] to the enactment of legis-

---

authorities only if an adoptee also registers requesting a reunion. In Ireland, the Adoption Board, through the issuing of original birth certificates to adopted people, in fact offer identifying information to them concerning their natural mothers. They do not, however, issue adoption certificates to natural mothers which would enable them to know the new adopted identity of their child.

[2] For example, legislation permitting the right to information and contact for adoptees has been enacted in England and Wales, and Scotland. In British Columbia, New South Wales and New Zealand the legislation enacted gives rights of information and contact to both adoptees and natural mothers.

lation permitting the possibility of contact between adoptees and their families of origin. As a result, in some countries, adoption reunions were now legitimated and facilitated by the state and recognised by the state and adoption agencies as an integral part of the adoption process.

To date, no legislation on search and reunion has been enacted in Ireland.[3] However, all 13 adoption agencies and the Adoption Board have introduced their own internal procedures in relation to search and reunion and as stated above are offering a search and reunion service to natural mothers and adoptees.[4] It is difficult to pinpoint the exact reasons for the dramatic change in the policies of agencies, though again the increasing numbers of requests from adopted people and natural mothers for a reunion service must have had some impact in making them aware that there was a call for such a service. In addition the fact that adoptive parents were returning to agencies requesting more complete information on their adopted children may also have had an influence on agency policy. Questioning by social workers as to whether the ethos of closed adoption[5] was a fair or just process for adoptees and birth mothers led to debates within agencies and among social workers about polices in relation to closed adoption and reunion.[6] Greater knowledge in relation to the life-long impact of adoption and separation through adoption was informing current social work practice and it appeared that the policies of closed adoption had not worked for an increasing number of adoptees and natural mothers. Information and studies from other countries were indicating that reunions between natural

---

[3] Draft legislation is currently being examined by the Attorney General.

[4] As noted earlier, the Adoption Board has just recently (March 2005) introduced a voluntary contact register.

[5] One of the implications of closed adoption was a presumption that an adopted child would never want to know about their origins and that natural mothers would never want to see or hear about their child.

[6] Within the Council of Irish Adoption Agencies considerable time has been spent discussing and debating issues of search and reunion: Council of Irish Adoption Agencies, Council Minutes: 1990–2000.

mothers and their children were happening and that to have the option to do so seemed to be what was being called for by the people most affected by adoption, adoptees, natural parents and adoptive parents. It appears that for all of these reasons the demand for adoption reunion in Ireland was also significant and increasing.

Preparing for Reunion

The findings of this study demonstrate that the work involved in preparing for a reunion was invariably an emotionally draining task and there were many issues from the past which presented themselves to mothers as potential problems. It is not hard to imagine how, for a mother who had not seen or heard about her child for periods of 16 to 40 years, the effect of hearing that there was a possibility of meeting would be overwhelming. In this study, in order to survive the years in the aftermath of adoption, relinquishing mothers had often to suppress their real emotions, placing them, as Goffman (1959) describes, "backstage" in their minds. They had, as described earlier, through various strategies of denial and emotion management, to silence their motherhood.

The work of denying their motherhood and by implication their child was a continuous process in which mothers had to engage as they got on with their lives in the aftermath of relinquishment. In the intervening years, as they met and made new friends, married, had other children, or moved to new locations, decisions had constantly to be made in relation to whether they should continue to deny the existence of their child or whether they could possibly break the silence and secrecy around their motherhood. Often they were like actors, acting out a role which hid an extremely painful part of their past. In maintaining the silence about their motherhood they had to undertake what Hochschild (1990) refers to as "the emotional task of consciously altering outward expression of emotion in the service of altering inner feelings". When describing how, in the aftermath of relinquishment, she could "never afford to get depressed" one of the mothers in this study described just how through this conscious altering of her outward expression, she managed to convey a different impression of her emotional state. When asked if she had ever let anyone know about her child, she said:

> *"No, because if you did, you would divulge your secret, you had to have a mask, the whole time, you were the happiest person in this world and your heart was breaking. But what could you do?" (Res 5)*

In preparing for reunion, mothers had to alter their emotional tasks and begin to let themselves recognise that they were indeed mothers to these children.

Despite a shift in attitudes towards unmarried mothers and the growing trend towards lone mothers keeping their children,[7] the shame and stigma which the respondents in this study had experienced as a result of their non-marital pregnancy had not been forgotten. As the years passed and attitudes towards single pregnant women and unmarried mothers became more open, the mothers now often felt a new shame in relation to having relinquished their child. Adoption was no longer the solution, or at least an acceptable solution to the crisis of single pregnancy. Mahon, Conlon and Dillon (1998), for example, found that women in their study on crisis pregnancy "rejected adoption because they did not agree with it" or because they "could not cope with it". These women expressed the view that they felt they would have bonded with their baby too much by the time they gave birth to consider adoption. They described how they imagined they would always be thinking of the child and wondering whether or not the child would want to meet them later in life. They felt they could not cope with these aspects of adoption or the aftermath they felt it entailed and so rejected adoption as a solution to crisis

---

[7] For instance, in 1971 adoptions as a percentage of non-marital births were recorded at 71 per cent; in 1981 this figure had dropped to 30.4 per cent; in 1991 it had further dropped to 6.6 per cent and in 1999 (the last year for which statistics are available) it had dropped to 1.93 per cent (Source: Adoption Board Report 1999).

pregnancy. For the respondents in this study who had parted with their child many years previously, the awareness of having been party to a process which was now no longer an acceptable solution for a mother, caused further emotional distress. It is understandable that when the reality of contact and the possibility of a reunion presented themselves, their emotional equilibrium was once again upset.

Upon receiving the news through the adoption agency that their child was interested in contact, respondents in this study described how heightened emotional states led at times to feelings of elation. Other respondents described how they were in a state of fear, and in some cases respondents described feeling out of control. Their experience was similar to that described by mothers interviewed by Gediman and Browne (1991) who said that "this period was one of extraordinary turbulence and confusion". Their emotional states were also akin to what had been found by Silverman et al. (1988) who reported that "when they received identifying information about their child, most of the searchers reported feeling "indescribably excited and shaky", "a catharsis", "fantastic", and "the end of mourning, no more wondering". Robinson (2000) suggested that for all natural mothers this is a time of "significant emotional trauma". In her own case she recounted how "within the space of two weeks I went from the heights of elation to the depths of despair".

In this study contact was initiated by natural mothers in six cases, and by the adoptee in twelve cases. What emerges in the findings is that, regardless of who had initiated contact, the impending reunion created great uncertainty for the respondents. They were concerned as to how the child might regard them, and toyed with ideas such as being blamed for abandoning their child or rejected by their child once they had met. Their overriding fear was that they would not live up to their child's expectations. These fears and speculations were similar to those described in other accounts of reunion by relinquishing mothers. Sullivan and Groden (1995) state that many of their respondents "commented on their fear of explaining the reasons for the adoption, and the

associated fear that their birth child would hold it against them".
Musser (1979) described how once a letter to her daughter had
been dispatched she was immediately "fearful of being rejected".
McColm (1993) records how "a number of birth parents, from
early years on, feel that the adoptee is going to be angry with
them, that they're not going to want to see them because they
didn't raise them, that the adoptee hates them and that they, the
birth parents, don't have the right to see the adoptee". In this
study, the emotional turmoil created by the reality of contact was
difficult for these mothers. Their thoughts in anticipation of the
impending reunion did little to ease their confused and emotionally vulnerable states.

Surviving the Reunion Meeting

Given the highly emotional nature of adoption it makes sense that
the real world of a reunion meeting would be, by its very nature,
complex and highly charged. McColm (1993) suggests that reunion meetings can be likened to other "rites of passage" such as
weddings and funerals. Like any major life changes, reunion
meetings are a turning point, and as part of the process comes a
release of emotions that were often, until the meeting actually
took place, suppressed and silenced. A reunion meeting is, in fact,
according to McColm (1993), "a launch into uncharted waters". It
is invariably a journey into the unknown.

It can difficult for the tone of first meetings to be comfortable
because natural mothers and adoptees are under severe stress in
anticipation of something which they may have always wanted,
but about which there are no guarantees. For all of the respondents in this study, the actual reunion meeting turned out to be an
emotional event which had many tensions. Their experiences
were similar to those which were remarked on by the respondents
in the study by McMillan and Irving (1997):

> No matter what the venue, the length of time involved, or
> who was present, first meetings are dramatic and highly
> charged events.

When arriving at the venue for their reunion meetings, mothers were often happy and excited, but alongside these emotions they were often anxious and fearful. Most of all they wondered what their child would think of them and what kind of an impression they would make on their child. In everyday life, there is a clear understanding that first impressions are important (Goffman, 1959). Whereas these mothers had *met* their child before, their child was at that time a small baby and they had no way of knowing what the child's feelings or impression of them had been. In the intervening years they had no knowledge of what kind of impression their child had been given of them. The mothers wondered also how their child might have fantasised about them and whether these fantasies were in any way a reflection of the kind of person they actually were.

When an individual appears before others he will have many motives for trying to control the impression they receive of him (Goffman, 1959). Natural mothers had many motives for wanting their child to have a good impression of them at the first reunion meeting. They wanted their child to believe and understand *their* story about the relinquishment process. They wanted their child to appreciate how difficult it had been to go through with the relinquishment. They wanted their child to forgive them for what they had done. And most of all they hoped and wished that their child would like them sufficiently to want to have a relationship in the aftermath of the reunion meeting.

Whatever the outcome of a reunion meeting, the actual event of such a meeting does in fact fulfil many of the hopes, wishes and desires of natural mothers. It goes a long way towards answering questions that may have plagued the mind of a natural mother for many years. When she has met with her child a mother can be certain her child was alive and well. There are also, however, difficult tasks to be accomplished at a reunion meeting. The natural mother's own version of the history of relinquishment and the reasons for parting with her child has to be recounted. For the mothers in this study, recounting this history was a difficult and emotional task, and even having done so they had no real way of knowing if their child believed their version of events. Neither could they be sure what their child really felt about being placed for adoption and whether they forgave their natural mothers for inflicting the status of illegitimacy and adoption on them. Whereas one respondent remembered her child saying "there is nothing to forgive", she also recounted how she could not accept this forgiveness. The guilt of parting with their child had been so intense for so long that it was unrealistic and improbable that they might forgive themselves easily. Cotton and Parish (1987) also describe how the reunion meetings for their respondents were highly emotional, stressful and traumatic. In their study, issues of guilt about what they had done also emerged for the relinquishing mothers at the reunion.

The end of the reunion meeting was consistently difficult for all of the respondents in this study. It seemed, in most cases, that despite feeling their meetings had gone well, there were many unanswered questions about the future. In the aftermath of the meeting the mothers still did not know for sure whether they had lived up to their child's expectations of them, or whether a relationship would develop. They were exhausted and happy, but fearful and apprehensive about the future.

Managing the range of emotions they experienced throughout the reunion meeting was highlighted by the respondents in this study as an exhausting and overwhelming task. All their adult lives they had been practising emotional restraint; through denial and silence they had developed a shield to protect themselves against further hurt and pain. The reunion meeting re-opened the emotional floodgates but they were still required to engage in concentrated management of their emotions in order to give their child the best possible impression about themselves. A mother might have been expected to feel only happiness and elation about meeting their long-lost child, but the respondents in this study were aware that it was not as simple as that. The complexities and consequences of reunion were clear.

Agency Service in Relation to Reunion

The principal aim of this research was to discover what the experience of reunion had been like for a group of natural mothers who had been through the process. As outlined earlier, since there is no legislation in Ireland which gives a legal right to natural mothers or adoptees to have access to identifying information about each other, the only way such information can be obtained is through the adoption agency which facilitated the adoption or the Adoption Board. Adoption agencies and agency personnel were therefore closely involved in the process of reunion through being the body to facilitate the making of contact and the facilitation of reunion meetings. Since mothers in this study had little choice but to have their reunions facilitated through an agency, how the services offered impacted on the mothers' experience of reunion were important.

One of the findings of this study and studies in other countries was that natural mothers perceived agency pressure at the time of relinquishment as one of the reasons which deprived them of any choice in relation to what decisions could have been made about their child (Howe et al., 1992; Sullivan and Groden, 1995). In addition, in this study the comments of respondents about agency service confirm that during pregnancy and relinquishment they did not experience agencies to be helpful or sympathetic to their situation.[8] In general they believed they had been treated with disrespect and in a disempowering way. It was with this history, therefore, that the respondents again became clients of the adoption agency, but on this occasion requesting reunion services.

The procedures in relation to how contact was made with a natural mother after many years of silence were commented upon by the respondents. When an agency approached the natural mother *directly* through a letter or a phone call, rather than through an intermediary (for instance a member of their family), such an approach was considered to be respectful and empower-

---

[8] Only one respondent in this study described how throughout the pregnancy and relinquishment process she found the adoption agency to be helpful.

ing. When respect for the confidential and private nature of the process of adoption and search was adhered to by the agency personnel it was appreciated, as not all mothers had informed husbands and families of the fact that they had relinquished a child. What was considered to be unacceptable practice by an agency was, for instance, when a social worker arrived unannounced at the home of a mother and made enquiries as to her whereabouts. Such a breach of confidentiality was experienced as disrespectful and brought back memories of the kinds of disempowering procedures which had been in place at the time of relinquishment.

Once the initial contact had been made with mothers, and there was an agreement that the reunion process would proceed, respondents in this study identified how, for them, the availability of a social worker to offer counselling and support throughout this emotionally difficult time was important. Mothers were spending vast amounts of emotional energy reviewing and re-working the past while at the same time trying to formulate strategies and plans in relation to the best way to proceed in their relationship with their child. The assistance of a social worker at what they considered this emotionally vulnerable time was appreciated. The opportunity to discuss and explore their worries and concerns was considered to be of benefit. The belief that counselling should be available to natural mothers at this stage in the reunion process was also identified in other research studies. Mullender and Kearn (1997) found that there was an overwhelmingly positive response from their respondents to the notion that in-built counselling should be part of the services offered when names had been registered on the Adoption Contact Register in England. Cotton and Parish (1987) found that when a counsellor was involved in the tracing and initial meeting, their assistance was seen as helpful. And Field (1990) reports that women who received some counselling before the reunion reported feeling better prepared than those who had not received such help.

When offering mothers assistance to prepare for a reunion meeting all the agencies who participated in this research appeared to have policies which encouraged natural mothers and adoptees to exchange letters and photographs prior to the actual reunion meeting. In their comments on this procedure, the mothers expressed how they believed it was a good idea to engage in correspondence and exchange photographs so as to give themselves and their child a chance to introduce themselves to each other before the meeting. However, when this policy stretched to social workers reviewing the letters before they were passed on, the respondents found this to be controlling, disrespectful and disempowering. According to the mothers, the agencies' justification for this policy was so that a social worker could be in a position to forewarn the mother about potentially distressing news which might be contained in a letter. The mothers' experience and interpretation of this policy, however, was that they were being "treated like children" and they questioned "why at this stage of their lives" they had to be subjected to such an infringement of their privacy.

This policy of reading letters before they were passed on was practised by three of the five agencies involved in this research. For mothers who had dealt with agencies where their letters were not read, there were no reports of information which had been too distressing to handle upon being received directly by the mothers. The need for an adoption agency to have a policy which results in their reading the private and intimate correspondence between two adults is questionable. To natural mothers who were at the receiving end of such policies and procedures, these policies and procedures were experienced as controlling and disempowering and likened to the manner in which agencies treated them when they relinquished their child.

All of the reunion meetings in this study were facilitated by a social worker from within an agency and in all cases the mothers recounted how the assistance of a social worker was offered on the actual day of the meeting. Again, as with the exchange of correspondence, all of the agencies had different policies and practices as to how meetings were facilitated. At some meetings, the social worker was present at the beginning of the meeting, presumably with the intention of introducing the mother and child.

At other meetings, the social worker met the mothers and the adoptees before the meeting and left them in private for the actual meeting. When a social worker was present at the initial stages of a meeting it was found by the natural mothers to be intrusive and, in one instance, intimidating. This meeting, which had been dreamed of and fantasised about for years, was an intimate and personal occasion, and not one at which most natural mothers in this study wished to be observed. Reunion meetings at which there was no social worker present appeared to proceed without any problems. Whereas the respondents stated that they appreciated the offer of assistance on the day of reunion, the kind of assistance and the manner in which it happened were not always satisfactory and in some cases it was controlling and disempowering.

When discussing the provision of counselling and social work services in relation to the facilitation of reunions, McMillan and Irving (1997) state that:

> Counselling does not necessarily alter the long-term outcome of reunion, nor does it change what happened in the past. However, with counselling, reunion may be prepared for, reflected upon and more safely negotiated.

Overall the respondents in this study were satisfied with the services they were offered in relation to the reunion process. In fact, it was only when agencies' policies involved procedures which the natural mothers perceived as controlling, disrespectful and disempowering of them as adults that mothers had criticisms. It is therefore important to consider that, for mothers, it is the *kind* of assistance offered which is important in the reunion process.

Chapter 10

DISCUSSION (3):
LIFE AFTER REUNION —
REFLECTIONS ON A LIFETIME OF LOSS

Reunion meetings are the starting point of a long process of adjustment to the new roles and identities which have to be embodied into the lifestyle a mother who relinquished her child for adoption. In the findings of their study, Silverman et al. (1988) identified four hopes and expectations which mothers had expressed as they approached reunion. Initially, and most importantly, mothers wished to know what had happened to their child and to confirm for themselves that their child was alive and well. They also wished to be able to explain to their child the circumstances surrounding the relinquishment. Finally, they hoped that they would have the opportunity to establish a relationship with their child and through having a relationship, they also hoped they might eventually find some inner peace and healing. The hopes and expectations of the respondents in this study were similar to those expressed by the mothers in the study by Silverman et al. (1988).

The establishment of a relationship between two human beings happens over time and imposes demands and conditions on both the parties who are going to be involved. Whatever the hopes, desires and wishes of one party, the co-operation and continuing interest of the other in having a relationship is essential for the relationship to succeed. In the immediate aftermath of an adoption reunion, whatever the hopes and wishes of the natural mother, the willingness of the child to reciprocate in the establishment and maintenance of a relationship is crucial. At this juncture in the reunion process a natural mother has no way of knowing for certain if this willingness to establish and continue a relationship is really part of their child's agenda.

In the beginning of the reunion process there are many questions about the parameters and boundaries that will apply to a post-reunion relationship. As outlined earlier, especially in Ireland, the concept and reality of adoption reunion is a relatively new phenomenon. In one respect therefore, the natural mothers of this study may be classed as pioneers of the process within an Irish context. Although as already stated there are no official statistics on the total number of reunions which have taken place since the introduction of adoption, the information available from agencies[1] confirms that it is actually just a tiny percentage of the 41,315 adoptions which have taken place since 1952.[2] As a result there is a dearth of information, knowledge and experience to inform those embarking on the post-reunion journey. For the respondents in this study, the developing relationships were like uncharted territory where there were no established rules or models on which to base such a relationship. Despite these difficulties and impediments, however, what emerged within the findings of this research was that, despite not having roles or models on which to base their relationships, 16 of the 18 respondents had, at the time of interview, an ongoing relationship with their child. These relationships had developed over periods of one to nine years.

The central question of this research was to enquire as to how natural mothers had experienced reunion and its consequences. The development of a relationship with their child was one of the most significant of these consequences. How the mothers perceived the workings of these relationships and what their level of satisfaction with how the relationship had developed was important in the analysis of their total experience. Within the interviews,

---

[1] Personal communication with various adoption agencies.
[2] Figures from Adoption Board, Annual Report, 1999.

therefore, mothers were asked to relate how, from their own individual perspective, the relationship with their child was developing and progressing. They were also asked to identify the main factors which they believed were helping or hindering the development of a satisfactory relationship.

Relationships Satisfactory

For the ten mothers who identified their relationships as working well there were a number of factors which emerged as contributing to the relationship being satisfactory. The first of these factors was that there was a patterned and predictable structure attached to how the relationship functioned between mother and child. This afforded mothers the ability to be able to have trust in the relationship and how it might proceed. According to Giddens (1991), what matters in the building of trust in a relationship is that "one can rely on what the other says and does". In addition Giddens (1991) suggests that in relationships which are satisfactory, it is likely that "one is able to rely on regularly eliciting certain sorts of desired responses from the other". When describing their ongoing relationships with their children the mothers in this study identified how, through knowing they could rely on having contact with their child at regular intervals, and feeling sufficiently certain that the response to letters and phone calls would be positive, they were empowered to become confident in the developing relationship. Through accepting that once their child's initial curiosity had been satisfied, their child still wanted to be involved in a relationship with them, the mothers became more confident in themselves. They also believed their self-esteem had been enhanced. They believed that their own increasing self-confidence and their more positive sense of self-worth, which had come about as a result of the reunion, was positively influencing the relationship.

A second important factor which led to mothers believing that their relationships were satisfactory was the acceptance by natural mothers that they could not and never would be the kind of mother they might have wished to be to their child. Part of this realisation involved accepting the child's adoptive status, and coming to terms with the fact that as a result of adoption, the child *belonged* to another set of parents to whom most likely there was a significant allegiance and attachment. What was on offer from the child was a friendship, a friendship which was based on mutual respect and acceptance of the others' circumstances and situation. A further influence on the stability of this friendship between natural mothers and their child was the existence of a good relationship between the natural mother and the adoptive parents. When natural mothers had had an opportunity to meet the adoptive parents and in doing so accept them as a reality in their child's life, it appeared to enhance the relationships between natural mothers and their child. In their study of the experience of children who were adopted, Howe and Feast (2000) also found that "in reunions which had the most rewarding outcomes, adoptive and birth parents met, and they too established a friendly relationship, much to the delight and pleasure of the adopted person". For the natural mothers, the fact that they were able to offer their child the comfort of knowing there was an acceptance, on their part, of the adoptive parents, appeared, according to the mothers, to add positively to the relationship.

A particularly significant influence on the relationships which were working well was the fact that a good relationship had developed between the child who had been adopted and other children born to the natural mother post-relinquishment. Mothers had often worried about telling their other children that they had given birth to another child who had been placed for adoption. As it turned out, however, in all cases where mothers had other children, the mothers' other children were accepting and happy to hear the news that they had an older sibling. The fact that the children became friends and enjoyed spending time together was an extra bonus, or as one respondent described it, "it was just brilliant seeing the three of them together". McMillan and Irving (1997) state that "whilst sibling relationships can be difficult, they seem to have a different flavour, they are less loaded with meaning". As with the siblings involved in all reunions, the siblings in this present study were free to initiate and develop their relationships based on what McMillan and Irving (1997) describe as "compatibility and relatedness". Whatever the attraction, the establishment of relationships between siblings appeared to bring, according to the respondents, great satisfaction to the siblings, and immense joy to the respondents. This study therefore confirms the findings of McMillian and Irving (1997) about the importance of sibling relationships, especially when on both sides there was a willingness to work hard at acceptance and to accommodate the adopted person.

The final factor which emerged as contributing to a relationship working well appeared to be an ability on the part of the natural mothers to have realistic expectations of what *kind* of relationship might develop with their child. Being able to come to terms with the fact that they would never have the "mothering" role that they might have wished, and as a result accepting the limitations which would always be part of their relationship, seemed to give permission for good and solid friendships to develop between the mothers and their children. A friend is defined specifically as someone with whom one has a relationship unprompted by anything other than the rewards that the relationship provides (Giddens, 1991). Through being aware of their own expectations and as a result of not making demands for rewards that their child could not provide, a relationship which was satisfactory for natural mothers developed between them.

In order for post-reunion relationships to work they would appear to need "anchoring features" (Giddens, 1991) which give the relationship sufficient predictability and stability for it to be satisfactory, especially for the natural mothers. Post-reunion relationships are invariably going to be complex and have many uncertainties. The factors identified in the relationships analysed above however, would appear to be factors which gave them some stability and anchorage. The existence of these features within the relationships would appear to be what gave the natural mothers the strength to develop and move forward.

Relationships Unsatisfactory

The six mothers who stated that there were problems in their relationships with their children indicated that there were a number of significant factors which they believed were inhibiting their relationships from working well.

Just as a patterned and predictable structure was important to the maintenance of the relationships which were stable, the absence of such a structure led to instability, difficulties and dissatisfaction. In this study, the existence of unpredictable and erratic contact patterns within relationships made it difficult for mothers to develop trust in the relationship and as a consequence relationships were having difficulties and faltering. In each case where there were unpredictable contact patterns, the difficulties which arose did so for different reasons. When meetings were infrequent, mothers often failed to negotiate the circumstances and occasion of their next meeting. As a result, in the aftermath of meetings, mothers were uncertain as to when or what the next contact would be and because they did not feel confident in the relationship they felt unable to take the initiative to instigate the next contact themselves. In other instances, broken promises by the adoptee in relation to previously negotiated contact arrangements also led to natural mothers having little faith in the structure or functioning of the relationship. A successful relationship "depends on mutual trust between partners . . . but such trust cannot be taken as 'given': like other aspects of the relationship it has to be worked at — the trust of the other person has to be won" (Giddens, 1991). In a number of relationships in this study, as a result of the lack of confidence on the part of the mother and as a result of broken promises by adoptees, the opportunity to "work" on trust was undermined. As a result one of the essential anchoring features for building a relationship was absent which led to problems within the relationship.

When natural mothers appeared to have unrealistic expectations of the *type* of relationship that would develop, or about how their child would be in the relationship, problems developed. Respondents in this category appeared not to have truly accepted the adoptive status of their child. This was demonstrated by an expressed and continuing wish that their child might, for instance, "move back home", i.e. that the child would leave their adoptive home and return to live with their natural mother. Some mothers appeared unable to accept that their child might not relate to the home of the natural mother as being a place they could call "home". Such lack of acceptance of the adoptive status was also expressed through an obvious and expressed yearning for a mothering relationship of the type that might have been only if the child had not been relinquished. When it became obvious that the child did not relate to such a mothering relationship and that neither were they going to return to live with the natural mother, mothers expressed disappointment and regret that this could never be so. They also found it difficult to come to terms with infrequent meetings, and in some cases resented it when their child brought a sibling or boyfriend to the meeting. Mothers appeared to believe that as a result of not being able to have the "conditions" that were important to them met within the relationship, it was never going to be satisfactory. Though these mothers could identify and relate to the reasons why such conditions could not be met, they found it hard if not impossible to accept that what they had wanted for so long from their child was not on offer.

On the other hand, in another two instances where the relationships were faltering, the respondents believed that it was their *child* who had unrealistic expectations of what could be offered by the natural mother within the relationship. These unrealistic expectations led to problems within the post-reunion relationships. Demands by the adoptee for a high level of unpredictable and intense contact which took no account of the natural mother's needs, commitments and wishes was a condition that natural mothers could not meet. In the aftermath of relinquishment, these mothers had moved on and now had responsibilities and commitments to other children and partners. The renewed contact and resulting relationship with their child in the aftermath of reunion was a relationship which they believed had to find a place within their present family and life structure. A child who was making unreasonable and unpredictable demands on their natural mother within the new post-reunion relationship had an extremely negative impact on other relationships. That their child acted in such a way was upsetting and created confusion for a mother who was trying to balance all of her responsibilities. At the time of interview, mothers were still searching for solutions to these issues in order to make their relationships with their child more satisfactory.

The final factor which appeared to be a feature of unsatisfactory relationships was the existence of a considerable imbalance of power between the natural mother and child within the relationship. According to Robinson (2000), "many natural mothers have lived with low self-esteem since giving up their children and it is difficult for them to become assertive". Respondents in this study appeared to be lacking in confidence in relation to what they believed they *could* demand of the relationship. When an adoptee did not contact, respond or react within the relationship in the way that might have been expected, the self-confidence of the mother was often not sufficient to take the risk of confronting the problem. This assertiveness in some instances stretched to not believing they had a right to even making a phone call or to ask for a phone number in order to be able to initiate contact with their child. Instead, when their child did not, for instance, make contact when they had said they would, natural mothers often berated and blamed themselves for their child's actions or lack of action. The reactions of these respondents were similar to those identified by McColm (1993). She suggests that some natural mothers never overcome feelings of self-imposed blame and guilt about how others treat them. As a result of this significant imbalance of power within the relationships, and the inability of the natural mothers to act as they might have done in other situations, the post-reunion relationship with their child often experienced problems and was therefore unsatisfactory to the mothers.

Relationships Ceased

At the time of interview for this study, two of the 18 respondents were no longer in touch with their children. In both of these instances it was the child who initiated the search *and* the child who severed contact.

In this research, since only the views of the natural mothers were sought, it is possible only to speculate as to why these two relationships did not, in one instance, develop or, in the other, continue after a number of years. In the situation where the child severed contact immediately after the reunion meeting, it is impossible to know why the child chose to do this. A number of reasons could be posited: perhaps the child's primary need for information and a sense of history was satisfied by the details given by the respondent at the one meeting; perhaps there was disappointment with the person found; perhaps there was never any wish to have a relationship. Whatever the reason, the consequences of this action were that the natural mother was again in the realm of not knowing what had happened to her child, a state which had been difficult and distressing for her throughout her life.

For the second respondent in this category, the relationship had been in place for four years before it broke down. On reflection, the mother identified difficulties which had developed as the relationship progressed. In her opinion, at times during the relationship contact had been too intense, and at times there had been conflict between her child who had been adopted and her other child. There were differences in social class and financial status and throughout the four years there had nearly always been an erratic and haphazard contact pattern. Some of these factors were present in the six relationships which were unsatisfactory, but in this instance they led to a termination of the relationship.

Whatever the reasons for the termination of both of these relationships, the reality for the natural mothers was that they were distressed and upset that their child had chosen to sever contact. They were again powerless to influence a relationship with their child, though in this instance it was through their child's actions that they were disempowered.

What emerges from the findings of this and other research therefore is that the needs, aspirations, hopes and desires of the principal players involved in the process of reunion are different and diverse and so it is most likely that there is in fact "no such thing as an easy post-reunion" (Gediman and Browne, 1991). As a result of these kinds of complications and complexities related by the mothers in this study, it is difficult to imagine how the path of post-reunion could be smooth.

In their comprehensive study of reunion from the adoptee's perspective, Howe and Feast (2000) state that the two strongest themes in the search and reunion experience for the adopted person were: 1) the wish to develop a more complete sense of identity and 2) the need to understand why they had been placed for adoption. For most adopted people the development of a relationship was a secondary gain. Within this research, the need of natural mothers to recount the history and circumstances of relinquishment so that their child would gain an understanding of their being placed for adoption was an important theme. However, their wish for a satisfactory and ongoing relationship in the aftermath of reunion was also of primary importance to them. With both parties seeking *some* of the same things from the reunion process, but on the other hand also having different priorities, it is perhaps inevitable that conflicts and dissatisfaction arose within relationships, conflicts and dissatisfactions which will in some instances be possible to negotiate, and in which in other relationships may continue to be difficult.

Post-reunion relationships between natural mothers and their children are, because of their history, disjointed and at times unpredictable. They are inescapably marred by a past that was not shared (Gediman and Browne, 1991). The history and sense of family that was taken for granted in other family relationships does not exist. A different kind of history, one which is based on separation and loss, is the foundation stone. If relationships are to succeed they will need to find their own "anchoring features" to give them substance and stability. The relationships will perhaps always need to be negotiated and re-negotiated to take account of a past that was filled with loss.

Mothers' Reflections on Reunion

Overall, the respondents in this study were reflective on how they had experienced reunion and what it had meant to them. As stated earlier, the majority of mothers, despite some problems, had ongoing relationships with their children.

Irrespective of whether relationships were going well, were unsatisfactory, or had ceased, *all* of the 18 respondents in this research stated that they were glad that they had had a reunion with their child. The greatest benefit of reunion which was identified by all of the mothers was that they finally knew that their child was alive and well. For them, just knowing that their child "was OK" was a great relief after the many years of "not knowing". The mothers felt that they had become empowered through having information about their child. Mothers also identified how one of the most significant benefits of reunion was their own enhanced self-esteem and self-confidence. They spoke of feeling "more fulfilled", "more confident", "complete", and "proud of themselves". They also identified how they "no longer felt inferior". Sullivan and Groden (1995) also found that their respondents stated that as a result of reunion they felt more "complete", and even when they were not still in contact with their children they had enhanced feelings of personal "security" as a result of having been through a reunion. In relation to natural mothers' satisfaction that they had been through a reunion, therefore, the findings of this study concur with the findings of previous research in other countries, all of which report that the majority of mothers were glad they had met their child. Comments such as "it enhanced their lives" (Silverman, 1988), "it was a positive experience and they would do it again" (Sullivan and Groden, 1995), and "they had no regrets" (Cotton and Parish, 1987) were recorded by other researchers as the views of their respondents about their reunions. Again, as with this study, even for those whose experience of reunion had not been positive, satisfaction was expressed about the fact that it had taken place. In their analysis, Silverman et al. (1988) concluded that, "even when a reunion was not a success, it had a very positive impact on the birth parent's life". And Sullivan and Groden (1995) found that "95 per cent of birth parents said they would do it again" irrespective of whether the reunion had worked out to their satisfaction or not.

On the other hand, it is important to note that when reflecting on their reunions, natural mothers in this study also identified how, in the aftermath of reunion, they experienced a different kind of sadness and grief which was difficult for them. As relationships developed, the impact of what had been missed through not having had the opportunity to take on a mothering role of rearing their own child hit forcibly. Throughout the intervening years, mothers had mourned for the infant they had relinquished. Now they were in contact with an adult they did not know and who had been nurtured and raised by another mother. No matter what happiness the reunion brought, they had missed their child's years as a infant, as a toddler, as a teen and in some instances the years of their twenties and beyond. Once adoption had taken place, the adoptive parents had been given an opportunity that was forever denied to the natural mother. In instances where natural mothers did not or could not have subsequent children, they were forever denied the opportunity of motherhood. In these respects, therefore, the effect of adoption had been to disempower these women for life.

A final feature which was of great sadness for the majority (14) of the respondents in this study was the fact that the first name which they had given their child at birth had been changed. Although there were no legal requirements within adoption legislation which necessitated this procedure, it was the policy of adoption agencies to encourage adoptive parents to choose a new name for the child who was legally to become their child through adoption. In many cases, even if the adoptive parents had wanted to retain the Christian name, it was agency policy not to disclose the name which the natural mother had chosen for her child. In most instances, natural mothers were not informed that the name they had chosen would be completely changed.

The rationale for such policies appears to have been to completely sever any connections with the natural mother, so that a new beginning, which was not burdened with the natural mother's history, could be created for the child. The effects of these policies brought great sadness to natural mothers in the aftermath of reunion. Besides the gift of life, it was all they had been allowed to give their child. They questioned why they had ever been asked to choose a name in the first place if the name they chose was going to be changed and ultimately denied. The implementation of this policy by agencies was experienced as insulting and disrespectful, and as one respondent put it "it took away the bit of dignity" she had about her child. This official sanctioning of the denial of the identity of the child which had been given by the natural mother by state agencies was a further example of the controlling nature of the procedures which surrounded the adoption process. The outcome of such policies ensured that natural mothers were disempowered and remained a hidden and silent part of the history of adoption.

In concluding this chapter, what emerges from the findings of this research is that no matter how good the experience of reunion, nor indeed how satisfactory the post-reunion relationship, it seems that reunion can offer only partial relief to mothers who relinquished their children through adoption. Reunion cannot change the past and give these mothers back their baby. For all the mothers in this study, some part of the disempowerment and the everlasting sadness which had been created by relinquishment remained. The true extent of the loss which had been experienced by the natural mothers through the process of relinquishment and reunion was best portrayed in the reflections of one mother who spoke for all relinquishing mothers when she said:

> *"You were never prepared for the fact that it was a child you handed up and what you got back was an adult." (Res 2)*

Chapter 11

CONCLUSION

As outlined in Chapter 1, the overall aim of this research was to chart the experience of a small group of women who had been through an adoption reunion, and through the recording of their direct experience to provide a better understanding of the issues involved in the process of reunion.

Historically, and to the present day, the main rationale put forward for the existence of adoption is that it will promote the welfare of a child. The security and permanency which adoption offers are considered to be in the best interests of a child. Whilst it operates within a legal framework, much of the influence for its continued existence comes from studies on child development. Knowledge and information from these studies has influenced childcare policies and practices in various countries, including policies in relation to adoption. The promotion of the welfare of a child is seen to be best served through offering a child a chance to be brought up in a family with two parents where their need for continuity of care, security and a sense of belonging will enable him or her to grow into a productive and healthy individual (Bowlby, 1979; Brodzinsky et al., 1990; Triseliotis et al., 1997).

A further rationale for the promotion of adoption has been, and continues to be, the demand for children by infertile couples who are unable to have children by birth. Adoption meets the needs of an adopting couple who have wished for a child and provides them with the opportunity to become a family. Legally, through the process of adoption the rights and responsibilities of adoptive parents towards an adopted child are the same as if the child had been born to them. Systems of closed adoption have offered adoptive parents, if they so wish, the ability and opportunity to hide or conceal the original birth history of the child and to parent as if the formation of the family had happened in the same way as if the child had been born to them.

The third significant and influential rationale for the promotion of adoption has been the societal response to a particular group of mothers who were believed to be unwilling or unable to care for their children. It has long been presumed, in many jurisdictions, that large numbers of unmarried mothers have been grateful for the opportunity to "rid themselves" of their illegitimate child and to continue their lives as if the birth and relinquishment had never taken place. In fact, this belief has only relatively recently begun to be questioned (Inglis, 1984, Wells, 1994; Solinger, 1994).

During the 1960s and 1970s, Irish statistics, which recorded extremely large numbers of adoptions as a percentage of non-marital births, would, if taken at face value, have appeared to confirm this presumption that unmarried mothers were eager to rid themselves of their illegitimate child. When the histories behind the statistics were not visible or available it was presumed that these women had been glad to be able to relinquish their child and resume their lives as if the child had never existed.[1]

The concept of motherhood normally radiates with permanence and unconditional love by a mother for her child. When this widely held belief about motherhood was contrasted against these statistics, there appeared to be a conflict between the actions of these mothers and the philosophies and beliefs about the normal actions of the mother in relation to her child. For this research the question arose as to why, if so many years ago these women willingly parted with their child, they were now requesting to be reunited with this child. Uncovering elements of the meanings be-

---

[1] In 1964, adoptions as a percentage of non-marital births stood at 77.6 per cent. In 1974, this figure continued to be high at 61.3 per cent. (Source: Adoption Board, Annual Report, 1999).

hind these statistics therefore became part of the focus of this research study. Previous research reviewed appeared to suggest that mothers in other countries had felt under pressure from state and family systems to relinquish their children and that they had not, in fact, been unwilling to care for their child.

Having analysed the accounts of the respondents in this study, a central theme to emerge from the findings was that for natural mothers who relinquished their children in Ireland during the 1960s and 1970s, it was *not* the case that they were unwilling to care for the children to whom they had just given birth. Rather the decision and pressure to relinquish came about as a result of the position of women, and especially single pregnant women, in the wider social and cultural context of Irish society of the time.

Despite extravagant displays of religious fervour, Catholic Ireland in the mid-twentieth century was a grim, inward-looking and deeply repressive society (Cooney, 1999). As demonstrated through the accounts of the women in this study, there was a particularly patriarchal attitude to women who were pregnant outside marriage. According to Walby (1989, quoted in O'Connor, 1998), from a woman's point of view the concept of patriarchy implies that there is a system of social structures and practices in which men dominate, oppress and exploit women. This leads, according to Hartman (1981, quoted in O'Connor, 1998), to a situation where the position of women is one of inequality and subordination, which is precisely how the position of women in Ireland prior to the late 1970s could be described. The state, as a key site of public patriarchy, was a major force in the promotion and continuation of such inequality. For example, until 1973 permanent posts for women in the public service were confined to women who were single or widowed; women already employed in permanent posts lost their permanency on marriage. Equal pay did not become law until enforced by a European directive in 1975. Discrimination against women in areas of social welfare legislation was not removed until after a further European directive in 1978. Legal access to contraception and, as a result, an ability to control fertility, did not come about until 1981 and this access was initially confined to "bona fide" married couples. Such a denial of equal rights, of equal employment opportunities and equal pay structures for women, the lack of access to contraceptives and the absence of a reasonable state-supported welfare payment to single pregnant women, would appear, from the evidence of the mothers in this research, to have been a direct influence on their having to relinquish their children for adoption. Realistically, as recounted in their narratives, as a result of the systems which were in place within the state, no other option besides adoption was available to them. Without the support of the state, of their families or of the putative fathers, they could not afford to keep and raise their children alone.

A key characteristic of Irish society has been the historically close relationship between the Catholic Church and the institutions of the state (Corcoran, 1996). The influence of the Roman Catholic Church, culturally and socially, has been considerable. In collaboration with the state, the Catholic Church has fostered a particular definition of the position of women (O'Connor, 1998). During the period when the women in this study relinquished their children, the influence of Catholic moral teachings on the position of single pregnant woman formed part of both the church and state policies and practices in relation to providing for their welfare. These attitudes stemmed from the moral teachings of the Catholic Church which were particularly unforgiving towards women who had offended the moral code in relation to sexual conduct.

Connell (1995a, quoted in O'Connor, 1998) suggests that although we think of gender as the property of individuals, it is also necessary to think of it as a property of institutions; often the practices and process within institutions may be more or less mapped by gender. Connell further suggests that one of the main characteristics of gender relations is the manner in which the structure of authority, control and coercion operate, i.e. who has legitimate authority to formulate ideas, to define morality or to set agendas. In Ireland in the 1960s and 1970s the representation of women in any of the hierarchical structures of church and state was extremely low. The subordination of women was achieved through enabling them to have only limited representation within these structures, and in some cases, especially within the church, no representation at all (Clancy et al., 1995; O'Connor, 1998, Cooney, 1999). The moral agenda as set within these state and church structures insisted that to be a woman who was single and pregnant outside marriage, was an offence against the prevailing moral code. To consider becoming a lone parent was a cultural anathema and a further challenge to the prevailing ethos of the time. These moral agendas and the resultant stigma which attached to non-compliance became the ethos of Irish society and often permeated through to it becoming the ethos of families and in many cases of single pregnant women themselves. This ethos also filtered through to the state and voluntary agencies from which the women in this study sought assistance. Within these agencies, adoption was believed to be the "solution" to the crisis of non-marital pregnancy. The results of this promotion of adoption as a solution to non-marital pregnancy took care of the welfare of the child who was protected from the status of illegitimacy, the needs of the infertile couple who could become a family, and restored the virginal, chaste and unsullied status to the woman who had been single and pregnant. For all of these reasons and because of the pressure they felt to conform to the prevailing moral agendas, the mothers in this study recounted how there was little choice but to follow the normal and accepted practice of the time which was to relinquish their child for adoption.

In the aftermath of relinquishment, and in order for the natural mother to preserve her status as a woman who had never given birth, the process of ensuring her motherhood was silenced was established. For this silencing to be successful it was necessary to have the co-operation of all the parties who had known about the adoption. Families who had been involved in hiding and silencing the pregnancy colluded in the continued silencing by never again mentioning the birth or existence of the child who had been relinquished. The mothers, who had been shamed and stigmatised throughout the process of pregnancy and relinquishment, erected their own status shields around their history which ensured them protection from this past shameful event. Adoption agencies, through their refusal to reply to correspondence and efforts on behalf of natural mothers attempting to keep in touch with their child, also complied with the norms of the day, which sought to deny the existence of the natural mother in the process of adoption.

The consequences of these structures and policies within Irish society resulted in it becoming the norm that natural mothers be disempowered through the process of adoption. What in effect happened for these women was that the variety of practices in relation to the denial of their motherhood, and the existence of their children, began to be taken for granted. This denial reflected and reinforced the patriarchal controls which existed around the relinquishment of their child and succeeded in denying these women a voice or place in the history of adoption.

In order to uncover and reveal the history of these women who, through their oppression and subordination, had become the hidden dimension of the adoption triangle, the use of feminist research methodology was considered to be the most appropriate within this research. Feminist research seeks to make visible the position of oppressed women and to give them a voice which will uncover their own experience of their social and personal world. One of the principles of a feminist strategy is that an interviewer has an obligation to be sensitive to the feelings of the respondents as part of the research strategy. The use, with their expressed permission, of mothers' direct quotations about the actual lived experience of relinquishment and reunion offered a previously voiceless and marginalised group of women the opportunity to be heard and to have their feelings of the experience recorded. The use of open-ended questions which asked them to reflect on relinquishment, on reunion and on how relationships with their children had worked out, gave them opportunity to be involved in the construction of data about their lives and to have their own views reflected within the research study. In relation to uncovering the histories of relinquishment and the effects of adoption therefore, the use of the core principles of feminist methodology within this study has made visible the fact that these women have actually lived a hidden dimension of our social history.

Feminist methodology also requires that the researcher be self-reflexive about her part and influence within the research process. At the beginning of the research it was impossible to be sure if the natural mothers would welcome the fact that the researcher was a social worker from an adoption agency. I was aware through my own work that many natural mothers believed that adoption agencies and social workers had not been helpful to them either at the time of relinquishment or at reunion. Through being honest and confronting this issue at the start of the interviews I endeavoured to ensure that mothers recognised that the relationship within the interviews was that of researcher and researched and that the power which a social worker might have had in other relationships was not present in the research interviews. The mothers were informed that I was approaching the topic believing that it was they, as natural mothers, who could tell me what I wanted to know. My belief was that I would hear from them what it was really like to have been through a reunion. The substance of their narratives confirmed this belief and the research offered them the opportunity to break the conspiracy of silence around their motherhood.

The centrality of loss for natural mothers within the whole process of adoption and reunion has been one of the most significant themes to emerge in this research. The contention that adoption is built on loss and that the effects of this loss became a significant life-changing event for mothers is evident throughout all the narratives. These findings are similar to the conclusions and findings of previous studies (Winkler and Van Keppel, 1984; Condon, 1986; Silverman et al., 1988; Logan, 1996; McMillan and Irving, 1997) and confirm that in Ireland, as had been found in other countries, the event of relinquishment created a distressing and life-long loss for many natural mothers.

The event of reunion eventually becomes, for some mothers, an integral part of the adoption process. What emerges from this study is that such adoption reunions will, for natural mothers, always be difficult, extremely emotional and highly charged events.

They will invariably be an event which will have a mixture of emotions unlike any other rite of passage in a mother's life. For mothers who relinquished their children in Ireland in the 1950s, 1960s and 1970s, adoption reunions are built on the foundations of a system of closed adoption, which, as has emerged in the findings of this and other research, have been disempowering and created enormous losses. Reunions, such as those in this study which took place in the 1990s, and those which will take place in the foreseeable future, are consequently taking place in the aftermath of a history of stigmatisation and the shaming of single pregnant women. It is within the framework of this history and experience, therefore, that women of this generation are, in the aftermath of reunion, attempting to establish and develop relationships with their child who was adopted.

When analysing the nature of the relationships of mothers with their children, the fact that only the perspective of the mother was available imposed limitations on any conclusions which could be drawn within the present study. Since the perspective of the adopted adult, the other party in these relationships was unknown, it was difficult to be conclusive about why some relationships were satisfactory and some were not.

From the mothers' perspectives, however, it was possible to speculate as to why certain factors appeared to add strength to the relationships. It appeared that mothers who were satisfied with relationships seemed to have begun to resolve their own grief about what they had missed by not having the opportunity to rear their own child. As a result of their own acceptance of the adoptive status of their child, they were able to demonstrate to their child that they understood the allegiance their child had to their adoptive family. Through accepting that the relationship with their child would be one of friendship, mothers were clear and honest with themselves and with their child about what was really on offer. They had come to an acceptance of how the relationship was going to develop. These mothers had achieved what Giddens (1991) refers to as the "art of being in the now". They had come to a self-understanding which was necessary to plan ahead and to construct a life trajectory which accorded somewhat with their own wishes (Giddens, 1991). Their main wish was to have a relationship with their child and in order to have this they had to accept the losses and gains that were the basis of such relationships. Through having engaged in the emotional work necessary for this relationship to happen, the mothers achieved, at least in some respects, their aim and desire.

On the other hand, mothers who were, as Gediman and Brown (1991) suggest, stuck with the "unfinished business and related emotional baggage which adoption produced" were less able to gain satisfaction from the new post-reunion relationships. Many of them continued to crave the mothering role, which was quite simply not available. These were mothers whose sense of their child as an infant had not changed. They appeared to be trying to cling to the past rather than develop a new perspective and relationship with their child who was now an adult. This unresolved loss was now compounded by the loss of a satisfactory relationship with their child. Emotionally they were not free to begin a new relationship which did not have a normal history and as a result was going to be difficult and complex. They had, for their own individual reasons, been unable to do the emotional work required to accept what had happened in the past and to come to terms with what was on offer for the future.

The evidence of this study suggests that adoption reunions and the resulting relationships will always be complex and complicated for natural mothers. They will always have had a long history which has up to now been silenced. They can never be separated from the act of relinquishment. The relationship involves two people who are related in the most intimate of ways, but who, when they meet, are total strangers to each other. The expectation has to be that these relationships will often be complicated and invariably involve losses and gains, especially for natural mothers.

Despite these uncertainties and complications, however, what this study also found was that reunions do offer natural mothers an opportunity to heal some of the pain of the past. Whereas the

theme of disempowerment in relation to relinquishment and reunion runs right through the experience of the women in this
study, it is fair to say that for most mothers the process of reunion
also brought some degree of happiness and empowerment to
their lives. It makes sense that the increasing self-confidence and
self-worth which mothers remarked on as being their personal
experience after reunion was most likely as a result of their being
able, at last, to be true to themselves about the fact of their motherhood. As their accounts demonstrate, this liberation of being
finally able to celebrate their motherhood both internally and ex-
ternally was empowering and exciting. The fact that their child
had, through being willing to meet with them, recognised them as
the mother who gave birth allowed them to believe in themselves
and emerge from the silence and denial which had surrounded
their motherhood.

The manner in which mothers were empowered was further
demonstrated in their ability and willingness to reflect critically
upon the reunion and be interviewed about their experience of
adoption and reunion. What also emerged in the interviews was
that they now felt sufficiently strong within themselves to analyse
their relationships with their children and to identify factors
which were helping or hindering the relationship. They were able
to contextualise the reunion in relation to the experience of relinquishment and the loss they had suffered as a result. They also, in
many instances, enquired from the researcher as to whether the
problems and issues they were experiencing in their own relationships occurred for other natural mothers. Whereas the women
had themselves engaged in self-reflexive work, this process was
further enhanced through the interviews for this research.
Through this reciprocal sharing of knowledge between the natural
mothers and the researcher, the mothers became collaborators in
the research project. They were also aware and supported the fact
that their information would be shared with others and believed
that through sharing their knowledge and experience other mothers might become sufficiently emancipated to do likewise.

A further way in which mothers in this study demonstrated their own sense of empowerment was through their having sought the services of a different helping agency when they had been dissatisfied with the policies and practices of the agency that had facilitated the reunion. In the post-reunion stage, they recognised that they needed further services but no longer believed that they did not have the right to make a decision about where they went for this service. This research, therefore confirms the findings of previous studies (Cotton and Parish, 1987; Slaytor, 1988; Silverman et al., 1988; Field, 1990; Sullivan et al., 1995; McMillan and Irving, 1997), which have concluded that reunions do appear to offer some healing to natural mothers, and that they also go some distance in empowering them within the adoption process.

In conclusion, the findings of this study have provided us with a unique long-term insight into the circumstances and feelings of a group of Irish mothers regarding the effects of adoption. The fact that adoption is not a static condition but a dynamic process which has far-reaching implications and consequences for all those directly involved is apparent from the detailed narratives and insights which have been provided by natural mothers. When the implications of previous policies and practices as they affected natural mothers have been analysed, it emerges that the silencing and secrecy which has surrounded adoption in the past has not worked. The oppressive and controlling practices of state and voluntary agencies have been proven to be unfair and disempowering especially to natural mothers.

At the beginning of a new millennium, the position and choices for a woman who becomes pregnant outside marriage in Ireland has changed. Only a tiny minority are now choosing to place their child for adoption. For the women who are choosing to continue their pregnancies and give birth, they do not believe they have to adhere to the norm of marriage and a two-parent family. For mothers who, many years ago, relinquished their children for adoption this change is both liberating and difficult. They are pleased that mothers are no longer forced to part with their child, but when they observe single mothers being given the opportunity to rear their children the enormity of their own loss as a result of adoption becomes clear. The fact that adoption is now considered to be an unacceptable option for a mother also makes it difficult to explain either to themselves or to others why they relinquished their children so many years ago.

For the mothers in this study, who have had to overcome the obstacles and stigma of the past and who have been brave enough to trace or be traced, adoption reunion has truly been an extremely courageous and noteworthy feat. Through being willing to talk about and share their experience they have increased our knowledge and understanding not just of reunion, but of the whole process of adoption. Their strength and courage in finally breaking the conspiracy of silence around their motherhood is now being recognised.

POSTSCRIPT

The mothers who participated in this study were contacted when it was completed in order that their wishes in relation to receiving a copy of the research could be ascertained.

In the ensuing conversations, two of the mothers whose relationships with their children were unsatisfactory at the time of the interview for this study informed the author that their relationships with their children were now very satisfactory. They had more regular contact and a mutually satisfactory relationship had become the norm. Both mothers expressed great happiness that this was the case. They also noted how reunion relationships will always be complex and how they may take years to reach a good equilibrium.

APPENDIX 1

Date:

Name of Agency
Address

Dear

I am writing to request the assistance of your adoption agency in a research study on adoption reunions in Ireland. I am registered for a Master's degree in Trinity College and this research will be the subject of my thesis.

The overall aim of the research is to gain greater knowledge and understanding of adoption reunion, particularly from the perspective of birth mothers. It is hoped that this knowledge and information will be of help to other mothers who are approaching a reunion, to children who were adopted, to adoption agencies who are involved in facilitating reunions and to the government who are formulating policies and legislation concerning adoption and reunion.

The study will be done by interviewing a sample of birth mothers about their reunion with the child they relinquished for adoption. The interviews will be recorded and analysed through qualitative social research techniques.

The assistance I am requesting from your agency is that your social workers would approach a small number of mothers to ask if they would be willing to participate in the research study. From your agency I would like to interview four women, if possible two who initiated the tracing process and two who were found by your agency on behalf of the adoptee. The reunion should have taken place before September 1997. All interviews will be conducted in strict confidence and all identifying information would be removed from the transcripts.

If your agency is in a position to co-operate I will supply you with copies of the attached letter introducing myself and the research study which would be sent by you directly to the mothers to ask them if they would be willing to participate. They would be asked to reply directly to me and there is no further involvement required from your agency. The results and findings of the research study will, of course, be shared with your agency and the mothers involved.

I am presently employed with SEEK, the adoption agency of the SEHB. They are actively supporting this research.

I would be obliged if you would consider my request as outlined and I hope your agency will be in a position to help.

I am available at the phone numbers listed above if you wish to discuss the request further. If I am not available please leave a message as to when it is convenient for me to contact you.

Yours sincerely,

Ruth Kelly

Encls.

APPENDIX 1A

Strictly Confidential

Dear

This letter is being sent to you by _____ Adoption Agency, on behalf of myself, Ruth Kelly, to ask if you would be willing to participate in a research study on adoption reunions in Ireland. The study is being done as part of a Masters programme in Trinity College, Dublin.

The purpose of the research is to gain a greater understanding and knowledge of adoption reunions from the birth mother's point of view. It is hoped that this knowledge and information will be of help to other mothers who are approaching reunion, to children who were adopted, to adoption agencies who are involved in facilitating reunions and to the government who are formulating policies and legislation concerning adoption and tracing.

If you agree to take part in this research, I would need to meet and interview you about the circumstances of your reunion with your child. The meeting would be organised at a time and place convenient for you.

The research is strictly confidential and information shared with the interviewer will remain confidential. All identifying information, such as names, etc., will be removed.

For your information, I am employed as a social worker and a significant amount of my work is to help facilitate adoption reunions.

If you are willing and able to take part in the study, could I ask you to fill out the enclosed form and return it to me in the stamped addressed envelope. I will then contact you and organise a time to meet.

Thank you in advance for your co-operation.

Yours sincerely,

Ruth Kelly

APPENDIX 1B

Strictly confidential

Research Study on Adoption Reunions

I agree to participate in the above study. I understand that a commitment is given by Ruth Kelly that all information shared is strictly confidential.

PLEASE PRINT:

NAME_____

ADDRESS_____

TELEPHONE_____

Please contact me by: Letter_____
                        Phone_____

I was contacted by _____(name of agency)

Please return this to Ruth Kelly in the enclosed stamped addressed envelope.

Thank you.

APPENDIX 2

Date

Name
Address

Dear

Thank you for responding to my request to take part in my research on birth mothers.

I am hoping to do my interviews in _____, and so I will contact you then to organise a time that might suit you.

I shall phone you towards the end of this month to arrange an appointment, and again thank you for agreeing to participate.

Yours sincerely,

Ruth Kelly

APPENDIX 3

Interview Guide

Date of interview:

Name of person interviewed:

Age: D.O.B.:

Single/Married/Separated

Other children

Where do you live now?

Where did you live at time of pregnancy?

Name of child adopted?

Male/Female

D.O.B. of child

Age of Child

Adopted name of your child now?

Where does your child live?

Length of time from when you contacted agency to reunion?

How long since reunion?

Does you present partner know about your child?

Do your children know?

Putative father involved?

Attend any groups?

Married to putative father/In contact?

Mother Searched   Child Searched

                              *   *   *

TELL ME ABOUT THE DECISION TO SEARCH/DECISION TO
AGREE TO CONTACT

TELL ME ABOUT THE PERIOD LEADING UP TO REUNION

TELL ME ABOUT THE DAY OF THE REUNION

IN THE PERIOD SINCE THE REUNION TELL ME WHAT THINGS
HAVE BEEN LIKE

HOW IS THE RELATIONSHIP GOING NOW?

WHAT FACTORS ARE INFLUENCING THE RELATIONSHIP?

WHO HAVE YOU TOLD ABOUT YOUR CHILD?

HAS YOUR CHILD A RELATIONSHIP WITH THE REST OF YOUR FAMILY?

HAD YOUR CHILD BEEN GIVEN THE CORRECT INFORMATION ABOUT YOU?

ARE YOU INVOLVED WITH YOUR CHILD'S ADOPTIVE FAMILY?

WHAT ARE YOUR FEELINGS ABOUT YOURSELF NOW POST-REUNION?

DO YOU THINK PLACING YOUR CHILD FOR ADOPTION HAS IMPACTED THE REST OF YOUR LIFE?

TELL ME ABOUT THE PREGNANCY

TELL ME ABOUT THE BIRTH

CAN YOU TELL ME ABOUT YOUR DECISION TO PLACE YOUR CHILD FOR ADOPTION?

WHAT DID YOU THINK HAPPENED TO YOUR BABY?

TELL ME ABOUT THE TIME JUST AFTER YOU PLACED YOUR CHILD FOR ADOPTION

AS YOUR CHILD GREW UP DID YOU FANTASISE ABOUT WHAT THEY WOULD BE LIKE?

TELL ME ABOUT THE SERVICE YOU GOT FROM THE AGENCY WHO FACILITATED YOUR REUNION.

HOW WOULD YOU LIKE THINGS TO BE IN THE FUTURE?

BIBLIOGRAPHY

Abramson, H. (1984) *Issues in Adoption in Ireland*, Dublin: Economic and Social Research Institute.

Adoption Act (1952) Dublin: Government Publications.

Adoption Board (1998) *Annual Report 1998*, Dublin: Government Publications.

Adoption Board (1999) *Annual Report 1999*, Dublin: Government Publications.

Adoption Review Committee, (1984) *Report of Review Committee on Adoption Services*, Dublin: Government Publications.

Anderson, K., Armitage, S., Jack, D., Wittner J. (1990) "Beginning Where We Are, Feminist Methodology in Oral History", in: *Feminist Research Methods*, McCarl Neilson, J. (1990), Colorado: Westview Press.

Arnold, M., Laskey, H. (1985) *Children of the Poor Clares, The Story of an Irish Orphanage*, Belfast: Appletree Press.

Barnardos, (1993) *Filling the Gap, Linking Birth Parents with their Adult Adopted Children*, Essex: Barnardos.

Barnardos, (1996) *Adoption, A Path Forward*, Adoption Advice Service, Dublin: Barnardos.

Batts, F. (1994) *For Love of Claire*, Dublin: Poolbeg.

Bennet, M. (1976) *The Character of Adoption*, London: Jonathan Cape.

Blaxter, L., Hugues, C., Tight, M. (1996) *How to Research*, Buckingham: Open University Press.

Bouchier, P., Lambert, L., Triseliotis, J. (1991) *Parting with a Child for Adoption: The Mother's Perspective*, London: British Agencies for Adoption and Fostering.

Bowlby, J. (1979) *The Making and Breaking of Affectional Bonds*, London: Tavistock.

Boyd, N. (1997) *An Analysis of the Representations of Unmarried Mothers in the Press*, Thesis in partial fulfilment of M.Phil., Dublin: Trinity College.

Bridgeman, S. (1993) *Adoption — Some Aspects of the Adult Adoptee's Experience*, M.Sc., Thesis, Dublin: Trinity College.

Brodzinsky, D., Schechter, M. (1990) *The Psychology of Adoption*, New York: Oxford University Press.

Brown, S., Limley, J., Small, R., Astbury, J. (1994) *Missing Voices: The Experience of Motherhood*, London: Oxford University Press.

Burnell, A. (1990) (Unpublished) *Explaining Adoption to Children who have been Adopted: How Do We Find the Right Words?* London: Post-Adoption Centre, London.

Burnell, A., Dagoo, R., Gorham, A., (1993) *Thoughts on Adoption by Black Adults Adopted as Children by White Parents*, London: Post-Adoption Centre.

Burnell, A., Fitsell, A., Reich, D. (1990) *Feeding the Hungry Ghost*, Discussion Paper, London: Post-Adoption Centre.

Burnell, A., Reich, D. (1993) *Making, Mediating and Maintaining Contact*, Discussion Paper, London: Post-Adoption Centre.

Byrne, A., Leonard, M. (eds) (1997) *Women and Irish Society: A Sociological Reader*, Belfast: Pale Publications.

Callanan, C. (2002) *Catholic Rescue and Repatriation. Irish Unmarried Mothers in England 1950s–70s*, Unpublished, Cork: University College.

Channel Four TV (1996) *Documentary on Mother and Baby Homes in the 1960s in England (St. Margarets)*, A Real Life Production for Channel 4, Producer: Jane Beckwith, London: Channel 4.

Channel Four TV (1997) *Sex in a Cold Climate*, Documentary about Magdalen Laundaries, Witness Series, London: Testimony Films.

Clancy, P., Drudy, S., Lynch, K., O'Dowd, L.(1995) *Irish Sociological Perspectives*, Dublin: Institute of Public Administration in association with the Sociological Association of Ireland.

Clancy, P., Drudy, S., Lynch, K., O'Dowd, L. (1996) *Ireland: A Sociological Profile*, Dublin: Institute of Public Administration.

Collins, P. (1993) *Letter to Louise*, London: Corgi.

Condon, J.T. (1986) "Psychological Disability in Women who Relinquished a Baby for Adoption", *Medical Journal of Australia*, No. 144.

Constitution of Ireland (*Bunreacht na hEireann*) (1937) Dublin: Government Publications.

Cook, J., Fonow, M. (1990) "Knowledge and Women's Interests", in: McCarl Neilson, J. (1990) *Feminist Research Methods*, Colorado: Westview.

Cooney, J. (1999) *John Charles McQuaid: Ruler of Catholic Ireland*, Dublin: O'Brien Press.

Corcoran, M. (1996) Church and State in Contemporary Ireland: Approaching a Crossroads. A paper presented at the Department of Political and Social Sciences, European University Institute, Italy, in 1996 (unpublished).

Cotton, P., Parish, A. (1987) *Original Thoughts: The View of Adult Adoptees and Birth Families Following Renewed Contact*, London: Barnardos.

Council Irish Adoption Agencies (1997) *Guidelines for Policy and Disclosure in Relation to Search: Adoption and Foster Care Placements*, Dublin: Council of Irish Adoption Agencies.

Cowling, S., Fitsell, A., Mallow, M. (1993) *Thoughts on Adoption for Adoptive Parents*, London: Post-Adoption Centre.

Curtis, A. (2001) *Open Adoption, Implicatons for Members of the Adoption Triangle*, Dissertation to National University of Ireland, in part fulfilment of the degree of Masters of Social Science, Dublin: UCD.

Darling, V. (1974) *Adoption in Ireland*, Care Discussion Paper No. 1, Dublin: Care.

Department of Health (1996) *Shaping a Healthier Future, A Strategy for Effective Health Care in the 1990s*, Dublin: Government Publications.

Depp, C. (1982) "After Reunion: Perceptions of Adult Adoptees, Adoptive Parents and Birth Parents", *Child Welfare*, Volume LXI, No. 2, February.

Deveraux, C. (1993) *Filling the Gap: Linking Birth Parents with their Adopted Adult Children*, London: Barnardos.

Doka, K. (1989) *Disenfranchised Grief: Recognising Hidden Sorrow*: Lexington, MA: Lexington Books.

Doyle, P. (1988) *The God Squad*, London: Corgi.

Eastern Health Board (1990) *Report on Search and Tracing*, (Internal Document), Dublin: Eastern Health Board.

Farrelly Conway, E. (1993) *Search and Reunion in the Adoption Triangle: Towards a Framework for Agency Service to the Adoption Triad*, Occasional Paper, Dublin: Trinity College.

Feast, J., Marwood, M., Seabrook, S., Warbur, A., Webb, L. (1994) *Preparing for Reunion: Adopted People, Adoptive Parents and Birth Parents Tell their Stories*, London: The Chidren's Society.

Field, J. (1990) "Long Term Outcomes for Birth Mothers Before and After Reunion: A New Zealand Survey", *Adoption and Fostering, Volume 14*, No. 4.

Finch, J. (1984) "The Ethics and Politics of Interviewing Women", in: Bell, C., Roberts, H. (1984) *Social Researching: Politics, Problems, Practice*, London: Routledge Keegan Paul.

Fitsell, A. (1994) *Sexual Attraction Following Reunion*, Discussion Paper, London: Post-Adoption Centre.

Gediman, J. (1988) "Giving up the Baby, Long Term Consequences for Birth Mothers", *Smith Alumnae Quarterly*, Winter 1988.

Gediman, J., Browne, L. (1991) *Birthbond: Reunions between Birth Parents and Adoptees, What Happens After*, New Jersey: New Horizon Press.

Gibbons, N. (1992) *Barnardo's Adoption Advice Service: Trends and Issues in Adoption in Ireland*, Dublin: Barnardos.

Gibbons, P., White P. (1991) *"Group Work with Women who have Placed a Child for Adoption*, Dublin: Irish Social Worker.

Gibson, C. (1998) "Semi-structured and unstructured interviewing: a comparison of methodologies in research with patients following discharge from an acute psychiatric hospital", *Journal of Psychiatric and Mental Health Nursing*, 1998, Vol. 5, 469-477.

Giddens, A. (1991) *Modernity and Self Identity*, New York: Polity Press.

Gilbert, N. (1993) *Researching Social Life*, London: Sage Publications.

Gilmartin, H. (1995) *Adoption Handbook: A Directory of Adoption Related Services*, Wicklow: Adoption Association of Ireland.

Glenn, E., Chang, G., Forcey, L. (1994) *Mothering: Ideology, Experience and Agency*, New York: Routledge.

Glesne, C., Peshkin, A. (1992) *Becoming Qualitative Researchers: An Introduction*, New York: Longman.

Goffman, I. (1959) *The Presentation of Self in Everyday Life*, New York: Anchor Books.

Goulding, J. (1998) *The Light in the Window*, Dublin: Poolbeg.

Granada Television (1996) *"Forgotten Mothers"*, Documentary on women who placed their child for adoption, London.

Greif, G. (1977) *Out of Touch: When Parents and Children Lose Contact after Divorce*, London: Oxford University Press.

Grotevant, H. and McRoy, R. (1998) *Openness in Adoption, Exploring Family Connections*, London: Sage.

Harper, J. (1993) "What does she look like?" *Adoption and Fostering*, Volume 17, Number 2.

Hill, S., Beattie, R., McDougall, M. (1999) "Conducting Qualitative Research in the Health Sector: Researcher Issues and Dilemmas". *Health Services Management Research*, No. 12, 183-189.

Hochschild, A. (1990) "Ideology and Emotion Management: A Perspective and Path for Future Research", in: Kemper, T. (ed) (1990) *Research Agendas in the Sociology of Emotion*, New York: SUNY Press.

Howe, D., Feast, J. (2000) *Adoption, Search and Reunion, The Long Term Experience of Adopted Adults*, London: The Children's Society.

Howe, D., Sawbridge, P., Hinings, D. (1992) *Half a Million Women: Mothers whoLose their Children by Adoption*, London: The Post-Adoption Centre.

Hughes, D. (1990) *What Can a Counsellor Do? A Personal Account of Counselling by a Mother who Parted with her Child for Adoption*, London: Post-Adoption Centre.

Humphreys, M. (1995) *Empty Cradles*, London: Corgi.

Inglis, K. (1984) *Living Mistakes: Mothers who Consented to Adoption*, Sydney: George, Allen and Unwin.

Inglis, T. (1987) *Moral Monopoly: the Catholic in Modern Irish Society*, Dublin: Gill and McMillan.

Inglis, T. (1998) *Lessons in Irish Sexuality*, Dublin: UCD Press.

Iredale, S. (1997) *Reunions: True Stories of Adoptees Meetings with their Natural Parents*, London: The Stationery Office.

Jacka, A. (1973) *Adoption in Brief, Research and Other Literature in the United States, Canada, and Great Britain, 1966–1972*, An Annotated Bibliography, London : National Children's Bureau, NFER Publishing.

James P.D. (1980) *Innocent Blood*, London: Penguin.

Kilkenny Social Services (1972) *The Unmarried Mother in the Irish Community*, A Report on the National Conference on Community Services for the Unmarried Parent, Kilkenny: Kilkenny Social Services.

Klass, D., Silverman, P., Nickman, S. (1996) *Continuing Bonds, New Understandings of Grief*, Philadelphia: Taylor and Francis.

Laslett, P. (1980) in Laslett, Oostervean and Smith (Eds.) *Bastardy and its Comparative History: Studies in the history of illegitimacy and marital nonconformism in Britain, Sweden, North America, Jamaica and Japan*, London: Edward Arnold.

Law Society of Ireland (2000) *Adoption Law: The Case for Reform*, Dublin: Law Reform Committee.

Lee, R. (1993) *Doing Research on Sensitive Topics*, London: Sage Publications.

Lefroy, L. (1987) *The Adoption Advice Service-Dublin, The First 10 Years, 1977–1987*, Dublin: Barnardos.

Lentin, R. (1993) "Feminist Research Methodologies – A Separate Paradigm? Notes for a Debate", *Irish Journal of Sociology*, Vol. 3, 119–138.

Lentin, R., Byrne, A. (2000) *Researching Women*, Dublin: Institute of Public Administration.

Leon, I.G. (1998) *When a Baby Dies: Psychotherapy for Newborn Loss*, New Haven: Yale University Press.

Lieblich, A., Josselson, R. (1994) *Exploring Identity and Gender, The Narrative Study of Lives*, London: Sage.

Lifton, B. (1994) *Journey of the Adopted Self*, Basic Books, New York: Harper Collins.

Lillis, M. (1995) *Adoptive Motherhood: An Easy Option?*, A dissertation to University of Limerick in partial fulfilment of the requirements for the Degree of M.A. In Women's Studies, Limerick: University of Limerick.

Loader, P. (1997) "Such a Shame: A Consideration of Shame and Shaming Mechanisms in Families", *Child Abuse Review*, Vol. 7 (1998), 44–57.

Logan, J. (1996) "Birth Mothers and their Mental Health: Uncharted Territory", *British Journal of Social Work*, Vol. 26, 609–625.

Lynott, P., Hayden, J. (1995) *My Boy: The Philip Lynott Story*, Dublin: Hot Press Publishing.

Maher, M. (1973) *You and Your Baby*, Torc Books, Dublin: Gill and Macmillan.

Mahon, E., Conlon, C., Dillon, L. (1998) *Women and Crisis Pregnancy*, Dublin: Government Publications.

Marshall, C., Rossman G. (1995) *Designing Qualitative Research*, London: Sage Publications.

May, T. (1998) *Social Research, Issues, Methods and Process*, 2nd ed., Philadelphia: Open University Press.

McCarl Neilson, J. (1990) *Feminist Research Methods*, Colorado: Westview Press.

McCarthy, M. (1996) *Remember Me*, Dublin: Poolbeg Press.

McCashin, A. (1996) *Lone Mothers in Ireland: A Local Study*, Combat Poverty Agency Research Report Series, Dublin: Oak Tree Press.

McColm, M. (1993) *Adoption Reunions, A Book for Adoptees, Birth Parents and Adoptive Families*, Ontario: Second Story Press.

McMillan, R., Irving, G. (1997) *Heart of Reunion, Some Experiences of Reunion in Scotland*, London: Barnardos.

Melina, L. (1986) *Raising Adopted Children*, New York: Harper Perennial.

Miles, M., Huberman, A. (1997) *Management Development: Strategies for Action*, 3rd ed., London: IPD.

Miles, M., Huberman, A. (1994) *Qualitative Data Analysis, An Expanded Analysis*, 2nd ed., London: Sage.

Millen, L., Roll, S. (1985) "Solomon's Mothers: A Special Case of Pathological Bereavement", *American Journal of Orthopsychiatry*, July.

Miller, G., Dingwall, R. (eds.) (1997) *Context and Method in Qualitative Research*, London : Sage.

Milotte, M. (1997) *Banished Babies: The Secret History of Ireland's Baby Export Business*, Dublin: New Island Books.

Morris, R. (1996) *Legitimate Mothers, Women and Adoption in Ireland*, Thesis in Partial Fulfilment of M. Phil, Dublin: Trinity College.

Morse, J. (ed) (1997) *Completing a Qualitative Project*, London: Sage.

Mosse, Kate (1996) *Eskimo Kissing*, London: Coronet.

Mullender, A., Kearn, S. (1997) *"I'm Here Waiting": Birth Relatives' Views on Part II of the Adoption Contact Register for England and Wales*, London: British Agencies for Adoption and Fostering.

Musick, J. (1993) *Young, Poor and Pregnant: The Psychology of Teenage Motherhood*, New York: Yale University Press.

Musser, S. (1979) *I Would Have Searched Forever*, Florida: Adoption Awareness Press, Musser Foundation.

Nic Ghiolla Phadraig, M. (1995) in: Clancy, P., Drudy, S., Lynch, K., O"Dowd, L.(1995*) Irish Sociological Perspectives*, Dublin: Institute of Public Administration in association with the Sociological Association of Ireland.

Norris, J. (1997) "Meaning Through Form, Alternative Modes of Knowledge Representation, Completing a Qualitative Project, Details and Dialogue, in: Morse, J. (1997) *Completing a Qualitative Project*, London: Sage.

O'Connor, P. (1998) *Emerging Voices*, Dublin: Institute of Public Administration.

O'Halloran, K. (1992) *Adoption Law and Practice*, Dublin: Butterworth.

O'Hare, A., Dromey, M., O'Connor, A., Clarke, M., Kirwan, G. (1983) *Mothers Alone*, Dublin: Federation of Services for Unmarried Mothers.

Ochberg, R. (1994) "Life Stories and Storied Lives", in Lieblich, A., Josselson, R. (1994) *Exploring Identity and Gender, The Narrative Study of Lives*, London: Sage.

Pacheco, F., Eme, R. (1993) "An Outcome Study of the Reunion between Adoptees and Biological Parents," *Child Welfare*, Vol. LXXII, No. 1.

PACT (1995) *Annual Report of PACT Adoption Agency 1995*, Dublin: PACT.

Parkes, C. (1991) *Bereavement, Studies of Grief in Adult Life* (3rd ed), London: Routledge.

Patton, M., (1990) *Qualitative Evaluation and Research Methods*, London: Sage.

Phoenix, A., Woollett, A., Lloyd, E., (1991) *Motherhood: Meanings, Practices and Ideology*, London: Sage.

Pierce, R. (1970) *Single and Pregnant*, Boston: Beacon Press.

Powell, F. (1992) *Irish Social Policy 1600–1900*, New York: Edwin Mellen.

Powell, S., Warren, J. (1997) *The Easy Way Out? Birth Mothers of Adopted Children — The Hidden Side of Adoption*, London: Minerva Press.

Raynor, L. (1971) *Giving up a Baby for Adoption, A study of the Attitudes of Mothers to the Timing and Finality of Adoption Consents*, London: Association of British Adoption Agencies.

Reich, D. (1990) *Working with Mothers who Lost a Child through Adoption*, Discussion Paper, London: Post-Adoption Centre.

Reinharz S. (1994) "Feminist Biography: The Pains, The Joys, The Dilemmas in Exploring Identity and Gender", in: Lieblich, A., Josselson, R. (1994) *Exploring Identity and Gender, The Narrative Study of Lives*, London: Sage.

Richards, M. (1981) *Two to Tango*, Dublin: Ward River Press.

Richards, M. (1998) *Single Issue*, Dublin: Poolbeg Press.

Robinson, E. (2000) *Adoption and Loss, The Hidden Grief*, New South Wales: Clova Publication.

Robson, C. (1993) *Real World Research — A Resource for Social Scientists and Practitioners and Researchers*, Oxford: Blackwell.

Rubin, H., Rubin, I. (1995) *Qualitative Interviewing, The Art of Hearing Data*, London: Sage.

Rubin, L. (1976) *Worlds of Pain*, New York: Basic Book.

Scholfield, G. (1994) *The Youngest Mothers, The Experience of Pregnancy and Motherhood among Young Women of School Age*, Aldershot: Avebury.

Seale, J., Barnard, S. (1999) "Ethical Considerations in Therapy Research", *British Journal of Occupational Therapy*, August 1999, 62(8).

SEEK (Adoption Service of the South Eastern Health Board) (1996) Policy Document (Internal), Kilkenny: South Eastern Health Board.

Shatter, A. (1986) *Family Law in the Republic of Ireland*, 3rd edition, Dublin: Wolfhound Press.

Silverman, P. (1988) "The Grief of the Birthmother", in: *Helping Women Cope with Grief*, London: Sage.

Skehill, C. (1999) *The Nature of Social Work in Ireland*, New York: The Edwin Mellen Press.

Slaytor, P. (1988) "Reunion and Resolution: The Adoption Triangle", *Adoption and Fostering*, Vol. 12, No. 2.

Smith, A. (1996) "Qualitative Methodology: Analysing Participants' Perspectives", *Current Opinion in Psychiatry*, 1996, 9, 417–421.

Solinger, R. (1994) "Race and 'Value': Black and White Illegitimate Babies, 1945–1965" in: Glenn, E., Chang, G., Forcey, L. (1994) *Mothering Ideology, Experience and Agency*, New York: Routledge.

Sullivan, R., Groden, D. (1995) *Report on the Evaluation of the Adoption Reunion Registry*, British Columbia: Ministry of Social Services.

Tovey, H., Share, P. (2000) *A Sociology of Ireland*, Dublin: Gill and MacMillian.

Triseliotis, J., Shireman, J., Hundleby, M. (1997) *Adoption Theory, Policy and Practice*, London: Cassell.

Van Gulden, H., Bartels-Rabb, L. (1997) *Real Parents, Real Children*, New York: Crossroad.

Van Keppel, M. (1986) (unpublished) *How Dare They? Women who have Relinquished a Child for Adoption, and the Tasks of Intervention*, Paper presented to 4th National Women and Therapy Conference, Perth.

Verrier, N.N., (1983) *The Primal Wound*, Baltimore: Gateway.

Victorian Adoption Network for Information and Self Help (VANISH) (1997) (unpublished), *The VANISH Resource Booklet (Draft)*, VANISH, Carlton, Australia.

Viney, M. (1964) *No Birthright*, Dublin: Irish Times Publications.

Wadia-Ells, S. (1996) *The Adoption Reader*, London: The Women's Press.

Wallace, J. (1995) *Unmarried Mothers in Ireland in the Middle Decades of the 20th Century*, M.Phil. Thesis, Women's Studies, Dublin: Trinity College.

Waters, J. (1991) *Jiving at the Crossroads*, Belfast: Blackstaff Press.

Watson, K. (1986) "Birth Families, Living with the Adoption Decision", *Public Welfare*, Spring 1986.

Wells, S. (1990) "On Being a Birth Mother", *Adoption and Fostering*, Volume 14, No.2.

Wells, S. (1994) *Within Me, Without Me — Adoption: An Open and Shut Case?*, London: Scarlet Press.

Whyte, J.H. (1980) *Church and State in Modern Ireland 1923–1979*, Dublin: Gill and Macmillan.

Wicks, B. (1993) *Yesterday They Took My Baby*, London: Lime Tree.

Winkler, R., Van Keppel, M. (1984) *Relinquishing Mothers in Adoption: Their Long Term Adjustment*, Monograph No. 3, Melbourne: Institute of Family Studies.

Worden, W. (1995) *Grief Counselling and Grief Therapy, A Handbook for the Mental Health Practitioner*, London: Tavistock.